WHITE BOY
SINGIN' THE BLUES

by
Michael Bane

DA CAPO PRESS • NEW YORK

Library of Congress Cataloging in Publication Data

Bane, Michael.
    White boy singin' the blues / by Michael Bane. — 1st Da Capo Press
ed.
        p.   cm.
    Reprint. Originally published: Harmondsworth, Middlesex; New
York, N.Y.: Penguin Books, 1982. With new introd. and photos.
    Includes index.
    ISBN 0-306-80479-4
    1. Blues (Music) — United States — History and criticism. 2. Rock
music — United States — History and criticism. I. Title.
[ML3521.B35   1992]   91-39729
781.643 09 — dc20   CIP

This Da Capo Press paperback edition of *White Boy Singin' the Blues* is an
unabridged republication of the edition published in New York in 1982, with
the addition of new photos and a new introduction by the author. It is reprinted
by arrangement with Michael Bane.

Published by Da Capo Press, Inc.
A Subsidiary of Plenum Publishing Corporation
233 Spring Street, New York, N.Y. 10013

Manufactured in the United States of America

Photos courtesy of:

2, 3, 10-13: Center for Southern Folklore Archive
4-9: *Country Music Magazine*
1, 14: James Luther Dickinson

Selections from *What Happened in Memphis* by Fred L. Hutchins are reprinted
courtesy of David Less; copyright © Fred L. Hutchins, 1965; all rights reserved
by David Less. Portions of a taped interview with Dub Jenkins conducted by
David Less are included with the permission of David Less; copyright © David
Less, 1981; the interview was made possible by a grant from the Youthgrants
Division of the National Endowment for the Humanities.

Introduction to the Da Capo edition

"On the wrong side of the railroad track
Where the people have nothing to lose
I'm the son of a gambler whose luck never came
And a white man singing the blues . . ."
                                        —*Merle Haggard*

There is a cinder running track in Brooklyn, in Red Hook, sandwiched between a crack war zone and what passes for a park in this particularly grim corner of America. The track is littered with broken glass and the small plastic baggies that define the limits of the New Jack world, baking in the summer heat beneath concrete bleachers. To stand on that track on a summer afternoon, to see the closed factories and the shuttered windows, the burned hulks of cars and buildings, the remains of cooking fires for the homeless, the sense of desolation, of war, of lost lives and dreams, is to taste despair.

And yet, despite it all, there is the music.

The 440 yards around that track is a walking tour of the in-

3

credible mishmash that still makes up the living heart of American music. From old Rolling Stones to new NWA, hip hop to street salsa to Ethiopian drums, rap to slick Luther Vandross R&B — in the midst of despair, the beat goes on.

Running that quarter-mile, caught in the backblast of ghetto blasters and the slick noise of stealth-black BMWs with their 300-watt walls of sound, the raucous energy of street musicians and — amazingly — even the occasional nostalgia of an *a cappella* group, the music becomes a seamless melange, a call and response that stretches effortlessly across time and distance, from the hunting grounds of mind-numbing poverty to the haunts of the richest in the land.

In the years since I wrote *White Boy Singin' the Blues,* popular music has steadfastly confounded not only its critics but, to a large extent, its audiences as well. When *White Boy* was written, there was no MTV, no Michael Jackson videos, no half-dressed leather girls writhing to heavy metal. Heavy metal music itself was still an adolescent male footnote; rap had yet to move from its home in the ghetto; Madonna was teenaged hot flash. The whole concept of *disco dancing* was still thought of pejoratively. None of us had rediscovered the 1960s (many, in fact, were still trying hard to *forget* the 1960s). Rock was in resurgence.

So what happened?

Surprise, surprise. The same thing that happened before happened again. Music born with fire in the ghetto loses its innocence on pop radio. "Legitimate" minority artists lose out to slickly packaged, emotionally gutted, funhouse mirror versions of themselves — Run-DMC begets Vanilla Ice — and the music press frets and wrings its hands. Cultures are stretched and twisted like so much silly putty, and the music is manipulated like so much laundry detergent, just another product on the shelf.

This is not news. Music has always been a commodity, and the people who listen to music have always been consumers. Like many other products over the last decade, music has suffered from a shrinking product life cycle, increased global competition, a fractionalization of the marketplace, a wholesale shift in the delivery technology, a second shift in production technology. The market has not only become fractionalized, but willing to regroup at a moment's notice — which is why, for instance, the top ten "rock" albums for a week can include both country singer Garth Brooks and metal icons Metallica.

None of these things is particularly "bad," only different. The star-making machinery now runs at triple speed. There are now thousands of Phillipses and Chesses, with their ears glued to this ghetto or that enclave or another Third World country, listening for the new beat, now grist for the machine. In fact, the machine is running so fast now that it's hard to find the raw materials to keep up with the demand — it's not surprising that there's so much recycling going on.

Yet, still, the engine that drives the machine is the grinding of cultures. And in the multicultural world that urban America has become, the old and new, comfortable and alien, snap and chase like dogs in a pack.

I think it's safe to say that the beat does, indeed, go on. White boys still sing the blues. Sometimes the blues are black; sometimes they're brown or yellow. Sometimes the blues are white, and the singer is a different color. But, for better or worse, B.B. King still sings on Beale Street in Memphis, where much of *White Boy* takes place, and that's something. Late at night there you can still go down to the river, sit on the bluffs and hear women's laughter and, in the background somewhere, the strains of a National steel guitar. Maybe that's enough.

Michael Bane
1991

Contents

Acknowledgments

The list of people intimately involved with this book is a sobering one, but there are two whose contributions went far beyond the call of either duty or friendship: Peter Guralnick and Mary Ellen Moore kept things afloat, and for that they have my sincere thanks. Others contributed almost as much, and to them, also, my thanks: John Morthland, Nick Tosches, Russ Barnard, Mort Cooperman and the Lone Star Cafe, Mark Pucci, Walter Dawson and David Less in Memphis, Nancy Goldstein at Elektra Records, Estelle Axton of Stax Records, William Ivey and Douglas B. Green in Nashville, Phil Walden, Jim Dickinson, Conway Twitty, Judd Phillips, John Mayall, Norman Dayron, Nick Gravenites, David Evans, Dr. Sam Floyd, Michael Goodwin, and many, many others. Also, a special acknowledgment and thanks to Vicky Stein, formerly of The Viking Press, who was in the trenches from the beginning.

9

WHITE BOY
SINGIN' THE BLUES

PROLOGUE:
WHITE BOYS

It is summer in New York City. Up and down Fourteenth Street the vendors hawk their wares—shirts and jeans and plastic coat hangers and chili peppers and *gen-you-wine belts that go 'round your waist two times, right here, right now, one dollar!* The crowds push and jostle from vendor to vendor to the easy beat of music provided gratis by hundreds of huge, blaring radio speakers hoisted on hundreds of brown and black shoulders. The radios clash and battle: salsa from Puerto Rico, reggae from Jamaica, chants from Africa, doo-wop from the dim past, Donna Summer from the disco future, rock and roll from now all meld into a single strand, a single beat.

The beat flows through the crowd like a curving, sensuous snake until every shopper, every cruiser, every blood with his box slung on his shoulder is unconsciously marching along to it. It is New York City set to music, a new *West Side Story* percolating up from the streets, a way to move, a way to be . . .

Suddenly there is a discordant note, a stumble in the dance, fingernails scraping across the chalkboard of the Fourteenth Street Symphony. A step is missed, the beat is lost, a vendor's mark slips away. "Shee-it, man!" All around, heads turn in an almost subconscious reaction: What is that . . . *noise?*

The discordant note streams from a radio speaker hoisted on a shoulder, but the shoulder is wrong, all wrong. The bearer of the radio is a newcomer on the street. He has short blond hair, cut in an almost military style. His acne is mixed with freckles, and his face is flushed from the steamy heat. His half-closed eyes give him the air of a sleepwalker; his feet move slightly out of sync to the music thundering from the box on his shoulder. He is wearing a white shirt with pale orange stripes and a narrow collar, all the buttons safely buttoned. The shirt is tucked into a pair of navy blue pants that end in cuffs just above the ankles. His shoes are black, spit-polished ROTC issue, and they look incongruous marching in the Fourteenth Street patent-leather-and-sneaker parade.

He is white, and the brown-and-black crowd parts to make way. The people in the crowd are smiling; two men elbow each other and laugh out loud; a little girl points, but the brave soldier doesn't notice. Deep in some personal musical revelation, snapping his fingers, he is lost to the real world, high on . . . Barry Manilow.

The Fourteenth Street Symphony is being disrupted by the direct descendant of Elvis Presley, the Beatles, Mick Jagger, Bob Dylan, and God knows who else: A white boy trying to be black.

More than any of us would like to admit, our lives are shaped by cultural signposts. We may choose to see our-

selves as loners slogging through the American wasteland, or as bright members of some social movement
dedicated to changing that wasteland. But either way,
we take our cues on how to dress, talk, and act from the
shifting, mercurial popular culture, which is based, far
more than we realize, on the culture of black America.
Look at, for instance, the increasing peacock-ization of
male dress codes. The current cycle was triggered by the
discos, and the discos were the ultimate commercial expression of black music, suitably modified for white folks.
Take a quick look at the wave of blaxploitation films of
the early 1970s, such as the classic *Superfly*, and you'll see
very quickly where John Travolta got his natty grooming
ideas for *Saturday Night Fever*. Disco fashion and style
evolved from the early 1970s' obsessive dealings with
black pimps and their ladies. Black culture has become
the most pervasive influence on popular culture, with
roots reaching all the way back to the nineteenth century.

The white imitation of black culture hardly comes
from direct observation, for over a century after the war
that freed the slaves we remain two separate and distinct
cultures, with every indication that the races will remain
apart for a long, long time. But as with our dream of a
Wild West that never really existed, white America has
created a carefully constructed mythology of the American black—the two myths are summed up by critic/au-
thor Nick Tosches as "Cowboys and Niggers." While the
world of the Wild West was based on radio programs and
Sunday matinee movies (and later television), our mythology of black culture is based on black music.

Blacks and birds are known to sing without prompting, and white folk have been listening to both for a long,

long time. And with good reason, because black music is different from white music on the most basic levels. "The Negro's type of singin' was the blues," said bluesman Willie B. Thomas. " 'Cause he had the blues." Whites didn't have the blues. What they had was European marching music and classical music, neither of which was particularly suited to pioneer life in the New World.

Black music, though, was tempered in the furnace of slavery, bizarre African rhythms fired by a gospel fuel that straight white music seemed unable to capture. The music was real, earthy, and soulful, and it gave us a window on a culture as alien and intriguing as the dark side of the moon. Here was a seductive world, as mysterious as the half-lit entrance to a classy bordello and twice as inviting. The blues cried out s-e-x, real sex. In black gospel we heard freedom and release, celebration and joy, never realizing that those were the very elements missing in the "real" world of black Americans. In fact, we heard a lot of things, and we felt a tug deep down inside. We saw—or thought we saw—a world infinitely desirable, which we could never be a part of.

The first time I heard a switchblade open was on Beale Street in Memphis, Tennessee, the Home of the Blues. It sounded sort of like a coffin closing, and it was followed by the softest of voices, a sweet black voice: "White boy, I thinks you're in the wrong part of town. I thinks you're lost."

I wasn't lost. In fact, I was exactly where I wanted to be. Beale Street—something of a cross between Sodom, Gomorrah, Hell, and Niggertown—was where the choco-late-brown ladies weren't averse to showing a little flash of thigh to a scared-looking white kid, where there were still hints of the blues and laughter trickling from the last of the old honky-tonks. This was where W. C. Handy found the blues and Elvis Presley found the music that was going to change the world. I wasn't lost, but I left anyway, quickly.

Yet even as whites shaped their popular culture around the siren songs of the blacks, they never really stole the music. Instead, the music became the battlefield on which the wars between black and white were waged. And, surprisingly, it was in the music of America that the most successful fusions came about.

The most successful and long-lived fusion is, of course, rock and roll. Rock has dominated popular culture for so long that it's hard to imagine our world without it. It is generally accepted that rock is a mutated form of black music, a white boy singing the blues, but the reality of rock is far more complex. In rock's antecedents—rhythm and blues, the blues, country music, black gospel—we find the continuous battering of black against white, forcing the music to change again and again. And in many cases, most notably the spirituals, country music, and rock, the offspring is greater than the parents combined. In short, black and white combined, assimilated, and the results quite literally changed the world.

This book is about that battlefield, and how the battles on it have shaped both the music and us, the consumers of that music, down through the years. It is neither a history of black music nor a history of white music, nor does it attempt to answer every question about or explain every trend in popular music. Instead, it's a look at the sweep of popular music, from the slave ships to the discos and beyond. We'll be spending a lot of time in Memphis, because it is the single most important city in the history of American popular music, the Home of the Blues and

Beale Street, the home of Elvis Presley and Sun Records, the home of Stax Records and some of the finest soul music of the 1960s. One would be hard pressed to find some area of popular music that wasn't touched by that city—its influence can be felt in today's discos and country honky-tonks.

It was in Memphis that the most perfect assimilation of black and white took place, even as the relationship between the races degenerated, at times, into an actual shooting war. It is the height of irony that the most important black leader in America, Dr. Martin Luther King, died within sight of Beale Street, where white boys came to learn to sing the blues. Memphis was the cauldron, the eye of the storm, the forge on which new musical forms were hammered, and we will look closely at that city to find out what happened there.

We will also show how the blacks themselves were accepted into popular music—though only on white terms—and how whites ramrodded their way into black music. We'll even tell a few stories about blacks and whites and music—like the one about Freddie and Alice—and maybe find out more about ourselves in the process.

Here's a hint: We are not who we think we are.

A HISTORICAL INTERLUDE

Memphis, Monday afternoon, January 25, 1892:

The day is cold and gray, and the old Civil War veterans who cluster around Court Square in the center of town are predicting snow. Along Front Street, crowded with its cotton houses and honky-tonks, three young women are walking. Two are sisters, Freddie and Jo Ward; the third woman is their close friend. They are all three in their teens, and they're wrapping up a special visit to Memphis from their home in Golddust, Tennessee, up the Mississippi River some seventy-four miles from Memphis. They are in high spirits, having just visited friends, and they are looking forward to the pleasant cruise up river on the steamboat *Ora Lee*.

The women start down the bluff to the river, then hear the clatter of a carriage. In the carriage are two young women, Alice Mitchell and her friend Lillie Johnson. Outwardly, Alice Mitchell is quite calm and collected, as befits the young daughter of a prosperous furniture merchant. Inwardly, she is seething. She is young and she is in love, and the object of her affections is Freddie Ward, who is getting ready to board the riverboat and go home. For Alice, this is out of the question. She is, as her friends will later testify, strangely enamored of Freddie Ward, and she will not allow her to return to Golddust.

"Here, Miss Lillie," says Alice Mitchell, tossing the reins for the buggy into her friend's lap. "Hold the horse." She hops out of the buggy and races toward the three women, being careful not to slip on the ice-covered walk. Inside the pocket of her multilayered skirt is the wicked length of a straight razor, the very razor her father uses every morning for shaving. He is careful to keep the blade sharp, and he doesn't know that his daughter has stolen the razor from his shaving stand in the bathroom.

The three women pause to stare at Alice Mitchell, whose eyes are locked on Freddie Ward. While the other two women watch dumbstruck, Alice Mitchell calmly takes the razor from her pocket, folds it open, and slashes Freddie Ward across her breasts. Blood erupts from the wound, and Freddie runs screaming toward the river. Jo Ward, recovering her senses, smashes Alice Mitchell with her umbrella (sensible girls always carry umbrellas), only to have the enraged Alice spin and slash the razor across Jo's left breast.

Spotting Freddie well on her way to the safety of the riverboat, Alice nearly panics, then musters all her strength and races down the icy slope. Freddie screams and screams, but Alice has her from behind. Alice throws her left arm around Freddie's neck, pulls her head back, and neatly cuts her throat with the bloody razor.

That done, she lowers the razor and waits for the police to come.

This is how the story is remembered in Memphis, when it is remembered at all:

> You've heard about Alice and Freddie
> All over this Memphis town
> Alice had her razor ready
> And she cut poor Freddie down
>
> Freddie's sister hit Alice's head
> It did but little harm
> Alice got up and cut Freddie dead
> While holding her in the arm.

"Frankie and Johnny" probably sounds better than "Freddie and Alice," although the sex of the two combatants is equally vague. Perhaps the city would just as soon forget two women who were "strangely enamored" of each other, especially when they managed to spill blood all over the levee.

The real point is that even today Memphis is a city cloaked in myth, cloaked like the heavy fog in the very early morning at Elmwood Cemetery.

ROOTS: THE
AFRICAN CONNECTION

They've all got rhythm.
—An early "truism" about blacks

In the beginning, there was the beat. It echoed from the Congo to Upper Volta, from the Ivory Coast to the heart of the Mali empire, across the length and breadth of what Europeans called the Dark Continent. It was a beat that stirred the body and made the hackles rise on the backs of the necks of khaki-clad explorers or the not-so-conspicuous slavers. It was a beat that slipped like mercury through the sticky jungle nights, and for those who could understand, it spoke with an eloquence beyond the comprehension of the fuddled white men. From the Yoruba of West Africa came the beat of the *tama* or *kalengu,* the hourglass-shaped drum that spoke with the voice of a man. From the Bantu came the sensuous voice of the slit-drum, a hollowed-out tree trunk with two slits that created two tones. The white men, upon hearing

21

their first slit-drum echoing through the jungle—probably announcing to the whole world their arrival—remembered Samuel Morse and his dot-dash-dot code and called the drums the "telegraph of the jungle." Soon no self-respecting explorer returned to Europe without an amazing account of the telegraph drums.

Across West Africa came the omnipresent beat of the drums, exchanging messages, marking the entrance into manhood, celebrating marriage and birth, easing the transition from the world of the jungle to the world of the afterlife. Farther to the east, where there weren't drums (and in the west, accompanying the drums), the beat was carried by stringed instruments such as the *riti* or *godje* (the one-stringed fiddle), the *kuntigi* (a five-stringed lute that was perhaps one of the early ancestors of the American banjo), any number of zithers, harps, trumpets, clarinets, and flutes, or, perhaps most importantly, the African voice.

The whole of African music can be summed up in that catchphrase about rhythm—they've all got it, the white folks said. If we didn't really steal the beat, we did steal the people, and it is with slavery that the true story of rock and roll begins. But before we touch on that peculiar institution, we need to take a look at African music and culture because an enormous amount of both took root and grew in the New World. Everyday things, such as the word "okay," one of the omnipresent words in American English, had their origins in Africa. As early as 1721 clergyman Cotton Mather had recorded three examples of African dialect that would later worm their way into the language, including *grondy* (many), *cutty* (skin), and *sicky* (sick). It practically goes without saying that the bulk of American slang can be traced to roots in

Africa. Even quilting—that most American of crafts—was touched by Africa: in the South some of the oldest patterns, passed from mother to daughter from the days of slavery forward, are a rendering in fabric of traditional tribal designs.

But it is in American popular music that Africa really triumphs. The segregationists who damned rock and roll as "that jungle music" weren't that far off base, for the beat that moves down Fourteenth Street in New York City on any given day is indeed the same beat that echoed through the jungles of Africa before the slavers came.

African music and European music look at each other across an almost impenetrable barrier. Marshall McLuhan in *The Gutenberg Galaxy* observed that much of Western culture was shaped by the invention of the printing press and the inevitable spread of literacy. As a consequence, we became linear in our thinking—*C* follows *B*, which always follows *A*. We have thus been trapped in a universe of the mind, the body being relegated to second place. After all, nobody in Western culture said, "I *feel*, therefore I am," did they?

European music—the music of Mozart and Beethoven—was very much a part of that linear tradition. It could be written down and reproduced exactly as before, and thus the nature of music itself was changed. Music retained power, but it lost mysticism. European music soared to marvelous heights, but at the expense of a certain magic.

Nowhere is that more evident than in the relationship between art and artists in Western culture and the rest of the world. In Western culture artists and their creations are separate from everyday experience. Art is permanently enshrined, and the consumption of Art, be it painting, drama, literature, or music, is an Event.

Not so in Africa—at least not with music. African music is a communal art, if it can be said to be an art in the Western sense. Music is not just something that the tribe gathers to hear every Friday night. Rather it is the glue that holds a culture together, a way of making sense of life.

It all boils down to a question of function. In Europe music was something to be appreciated, enjoyed, *consumed,* like any other commodity. At its best—which was very good indeed—it offered a glimpse into a universe of the senses. At its worst, it was at least entertaining.

In Africa music was a part of day-to-day life, used to send messages, to aid in preparing food, to assure luck on the hunt, and for any number of more significant magical purposes. Francis Bebey, in his book *African Music: A People's Art,* says, "African musicians do not seek to combine sounds in a manner pleasing to the ear. Their aim is simply to express life in all of its aspects through a medium of sound." In fact, some African peoples didn't even have a word in their language for "music" until they came under Western influence. Music was so much a part of life that they saw no reason to call it by a special name. The nature of African languages is so tied to shifting tones that musical instruments actually speak—that is, they are heard and understood by members of a particular tribe just as if an individual were talking. The reality of the talking instruments is far more impressive than the "jungle telegraph." The difference between the spoken language and the sung language, individual language and the language of the musical instruments, is slight indeed. In fact, there is very little completely "instrumental" music in traditional African culture.

Is it any surprise, then, that in a culture where music was a part of everybody's life the people both shaped and were shaped by the beat, the ever-present sense of rhythm? Where there were no drums, the people found other outlets for the rhythm—stamping their feet, clapping, ringing bells, moving to it. Africans participated in their music to an extent that would have appalled the average European, who was accustomed to answering in a chorus or with an instrument when the song leader played or sang a phrase, or joining in with complicated harmonies. African music touched both the body and soul, and touched them on a level that was all but forgotten in Europe.

Then the slave ships came, and the people found themselves unwillingly transplanted to the blank slate that was America. The first thing they found out was that being a slave meant forsaking every vestige of Africa, for white America wanted docile workers, not a strange new culture. It wasn't enough to be a slave, it was necessary to become an *American* slave.

When the blacks arrived, America had little of what could be considerd a "folk" culture—aside from the American Indian culture that was being exterminated by the newly arrived Europeans. Bits and pieces of the English and European folk traditions had come over with the settlers, and the New World was beginning to twist those traditions into something unique. But it was the arrival of the blacks in their chains that signaled the birth of American folk culture. As early as 1746 an English visitor to the Colonies was appalled to find that young children of both races were allowed to play together and that young whites were speaking the pidgin English of the Africans. Where, the visitor moaned, will it all end?

What had to go were those damn drums! At first the slave owners couldn't have cared less—a drum is a drum is a drum. But African drums talked, and pretty soon the air between plantations was thick with everything from gossip to plans for insurrection. It didn't take the masters long to figure out that these drums weren't the same kind of drums used in local orchestras, and by the late 1700s the slaves had been forbidden to play the drum.

"It is ironic," wrote Ortiz M. Walton in *Music: Black, White & Blue*, "that these laws against the use of drums during the slave era . . . account for the single most important development of Afro-American music. . . . The enforcement of the anti-drum laws in the United States made it necessary to transfer the function of the drum to the hands, feet, and body by way of the Spirituals during the slave era and by way of instrumental music after the Civil War in the new form of black music called Jazz."

The beat went on.

In the deadening world of the fields music became more important than ever. All other aspects of African culture were denied the slave—religion, modes of dress, even family units were totally destroyed, replaced by the white man's Christianity, the white man's work clothes, and the "extended family" of the plantation. But the white masters couldn't shake the vision of the happy black children dancing in the fields. So, having taken away the drum—the evil, satanic device by which bad slaves spread their rot—the master was content to leave the darkies the rest of their entertainment.

That entertainment became an instrumental tool for survival. Slaves in the field sang work songs, "field hollers"—one of the basic ingredients of the blues—which took the place of the drums in transmitting messages from plantation to plantation. More importantly, the field hollers and the call-response songs sung in the field held the group together in the face of vicious oppression, as well as transmitted a portion of the group's African heritage. Utilizing the many subtle tricks and techniques of his musical background, the slave could take the most innocuous song and fill it with a wealth of information, most of it totally beyond the understanding of the masters.

Thus little by little the African influence percolated through American society. In a sense, the isolation of blacks on the plantation preserved the African connection until after the Civil War, when the former slaves made their way to the cities, only to find an altogether different form of slavery.

"Some people will tell you that the root form of American music is exclusively black," said musicologist Brian Guinle, who has spent years in the Mississippi Delta searching for the most African forms of black music. Some of the drum and fife music he has recorded can make the hair on the nape of your neck stand, just as it did on the necks of the first European explorers. "The music isn't exclusively black. It's a merging of the European and African cultures into a purely American culture. But you've still got the black beat, and you can still dance to it. The basic beat, even in the Mississippi Delta, is still African."

ROOTS: JESUS IN
BLACK AND WHITE

*There is nothing more futile, more completely stupid, than a negro's
ideas. He will talk for two hours about a musquito, about the
buttons on his coat, or the length of his nails.*
     —from a French traveler's journal, circa 1855

*Negro and white spirituals share similar Biblical symbolism, it is
true, but, in examining the now extensive collections of white spirituals we have yet to find any songs with the explicit sorrow over
the actual woes of this world, with the explicit anger against oppression, and with the ringing cries for freedom to be discoverd in
the Negro songs.*   —*The Folk Songs of North America*
                    by Alan Lomax

In all of American music there is no more awesome or
more influential and moving body of work than the
Negro "spirituals," what W. E. B. DuBois called the "sorrow songs," the religious hymns of the black slaves. These
sorrow songs are at the very root of most forms of Amer-

28

ican music—gospel, jazz, the blues, rock, soul, rhythm
and blues, even disco. There are probably very few
Americans who are not familiar with at least the best
known of the spirituals—"Steal Away," "Swing Low,
Sweet Chariot," "A Poor Wayfaring Stranger" (or "Pil-
grim's Song").

Even today, almost two centuries after their composition, the spirituals still have the power to jerk the listener
inside out, to give him a slave's-eye view of a world where
family and friends are lost on the auction block and the
very limits of the universe are bounded by the outer rim
of the plantation.

Unlike the music that would follow, such as gospel and
even the blues, the spirituals found little to celebrate. A
slave's life was unrelenting and unforgiving, with little or
no hope for change. The white man's religion, Christianity, offered some hope for relief in the by and by, but
even *that* was far removed from a sure thing, as this scrap
of doggerel collected by blues authority Paul Oliver painfully shows:

> White man use a whip
> White man use a trigger
> But the Bible and Jesus
> Made a slave of the nigger . . .

But the spirituals served a far more important purpose
than simply expressing, however eloquently, the melan-
cholia of an enslaved race. With the drum (and horns in
Mississippi) banned as methods of communication, the
spirituals became coded signals from slave to slave, the
new jungle telegraph. In fact, "Steal Away," certainly
one of the most famous and cherished of all spirituals, is

attributed to the slave Nat Turner, whose rebellion on August 21, 1831, cost him and his followers (as well as some sixty-odd whites) their lives and marked a major turning point in the history of black and white America. The beautiful, haunting lyrics of "Steal Away" were a signal to the other slaves to "steal away" to a secret meeting, to help plan the insurrection. As the white "massas" in Southampton County, Virginia, listened to the spiritual, secure in the knowledge that the "happy children" had accepted Jesus Christ as their Lord and Savior and therefore could hardly be up to any mischief, the slaves themselves were planning what would become known as "the massacre."

Although the lyrics of the spirituals leaned heavily on biblical terminology, the songs helped to preserve a major segment of African culture, that of the secret meeting of the cult. Along with their music, one of the most important customs Africans carried to the New World on the slave ships was the secret tribal meeting, a gathering (usually around midnight) of the men of the tribe for worship, dancing, induction into manhood, marriages, storytelling, and in general the transmission of the oral heritage of the tribe. In the New World the African cult meeting became, if anything, more important. As the slaveholders worked to break down the bonds of tribe and family by ruthlessly selling the Africans as if they were cattle, the secret meeting took the place of both, giving the newly arrived Africans the strength to face the rigors of slavery. Later the meetings served to introduce the slaves to Christianity and to help them plan rebellions and then escapes through the underground railroad.

The spirituals themselves were used to transmit all manner of information, from which massa was treating his slaves well, to specific routes for escape, to a generalized hope that soon the slave would be delivered into "Sweet Canaan." As former slave and ardent abolitionist Frederick Douglass pointed out in his autobiography, "The North was our Canaan."

The spirituals were also used to transmit information about the successes of the American Colonization Society, which, in the early 1800s, founded a colony of emancipated ex-slaves in Liberia. Each action by the Society, according to Dr. Miles Mark Fisher in his *Negro Slave Songs in the United States*, resulted in a wealth of spirituals describing the good life in Africa and expressing the hopes of the blacks that they would soon be "crossing over" to the colony.

The acceptance of Christianity at face value was something else again. Along with his drums and his freedom, the African had been forced to give up his religion, which was deemed too primitive, too satanic, too vigorous for a beast of burden. As a result (and because of vast efforts by northern evangelists), the slaves were offered Christianity, which they appeared to accept wholeheartedly. But the African was on speaking terms with his gods; like the music, the gods were a part of everyday life, presiding over all events, good and evil. They were worshiped with music and dance, with shouts and shakes.

The One True God of the Puritans, though, didn't much hold with shouting and shaking or anything that had to do with the body. This new God was accessible only through ministers. The new religion also introduced an element of *unworldliness* that was totally alien to the African. Be patient, the new religion said, your reward is not in this world (hence the bit of verse quoted earlier). Do your best in this life, Christianity told the black; be a *good* slave and your lot will be better in the next.

While the slaves accepted this otherworldliness on the surface, there is evidence that, at least until Nat Turner's rebellion, they didn't take heaven all that seriously. In fact, Dr. Fisher finds much evidence that Africa was the heaven being sung about, and that there was a pervasive belief in the slave communities that after death, rather than waking up in front of the Pearly Gates, the resurrected slave would wake up in Africa. After all, the African culture from which the blacks had been ripped was far more ancient than the New World culture to which they'd been delivered, and that African culture was deeply rooted in a day-to-day, live-life-as-it-comes tradition. Obviously, such a tradition would die hard.

It began dying with Nat Turner. The failure of his rebellion kicked the struts out from under the idea of organized revolt, and from that time forward the underground railroad became the route to the Promised Land. Every year it transported some two thousand slaves north, into Canaan. The other result of the failure of the Turner rebellion was that the more conservative blacks gained control over the militants, and the operative philosophy in the black community became bow and scrape to the whites in order to survive. Ironically, the lot of the slave did improve measurably, at least according to the extensive studies of Dr. Fisher. After the Turner revolt, the spirituals became more, well, spiritual, less concerned with day-to-day happenings and more engaged with human dignity and the ultimate release of the African people from bondage.

Where did the spirituals come from?

While the answer might seem simple—from the slaves— a horde of researchers has more or less proved otherwise.

Because researchers, from the 1800s to the present, carried their own particular biases, too many found what they were hoping to find—which happens to be a special demon for people who write about music, whether Bach or Chuck Berry. In fact, the spirituals were rooted in the religious music of poor rural whites, which was adapted by the slaves, molded according to their African tradition, and finally written down, codified, and published by whites. Then the music was sold to everyone.

The single largest influence on black spirituals was the songs of the white "born-again" revivalism of the early-nineteenth century. Tent preachers went all across the land exhorting people to come forward and be saved. At these camp revivals people shouted and sang and spoke in "tongues," and generally worked themselves into a frenzy we can see reflected in the Evangelical movement of the past few years. Revivalism reached its peak in the southern uplands, away from the sticky one-crop plantations along the tidewater.

But the uplands were not without slaves. In fact, as one nineteenth-century historian pointed out, the people of the uplands, with their small plantations and farms, were actually in closer contact with their slaves than the aristocratic massas of the tidewater, who were often insulated from their field hands. So the revival songs of the white South became part of the oral tradition of the black slave, transmitted across the plantations by the singing telegraph. The raw material of the revival songs was twisted and changed by the demands of the African cults and the necessity for secret communication. One of the hardest things to grasp in these days of records and sheet music and "why don't they sound the same in concert as they do on the radio?" is that the spirituals were constantly evolving, the words and melodies changing to suit the situation and the needs of the singer. In Africa music wasn't something that was written down and preserved: it served a day-to-day function. It was the linear-minded white man who first thought of writing down the spirituals to keep them "pure," so the darkies couldn't screw them up anymore.

Reading over the music of the southern revival camps, one gets an eerie feeling. The music—indeed, the whole network of the tent revivals—was drastically different from the church music that preceded it. The emphasis on release, the accompanying shouting and shaking and dancing, the call-response nature of the singing, all have a vaguely familiar ring. Communal singing, usually call-response; use of music in a magic rite; rhythmic shaking and dancing; shouts and other spontaneous noises . . . sounds like African music.

"Negro entered into White man," wrote historian W. C. Cash in his *Mind of the South,* "as profoundly as White man entered into Negro." By the time of the two huge revival movements in the mid-eighteenth and early-nineteenth centuries, the slave with his African culture was an established part of the American landscape. And the white man, already being molded by the harsh life of the New World, looked at that culture and saw some things he liked, some things that would fit into his life, and without further ado he appropriated those things. American music was off and running.

The early white Americans needed *something* to bring relief. They had carried their old religion to America with them, but that religion was about as suited to the New World as the proverbial teats on a boar. Puritanism started out as the brave new religion for the brave new world, but it found it almost impossible to escape its Anglican roots. It was the quintessential European religion—everything was governed by rules, every tiny aspect of day-to-day life had been thought out and the appropriate action dictated. All things, including slavery, the eradication of the Indians, and the American Revolution, were explained by reason. Puritanism was the triumph of the mind over the body. Is it any wonder that the Africans, with their overt emphasis on the body, were considered little better than cattle?

Into this staid, ordered—boring—world came the first genuine hellfire-and-brimstone evangelist, George Whitefield. Whitefield came over from England in 1740 and began whipping up the congregations in what became the tried-and-true manner. He gave them a taste of the furnace, and then jerked them back from the brink of hell with the promise of personal salvation at the hands of Jesus Lord and Savior.

After years of sitting on rock-hard benches listening to the monotonous droning of their Puritan ministers, the people were electrified. Pretty soon revivalism became a spreading fire—the Great Awakening. One of the very first by-products of the Great Awakening was song. People were voracious for music, and the leaders of the movement began reprocessing folk songs from across the ocean, tavern doggerel, and anything else they could lay their hands on into sacred songs to satisfy the demand.

By the late 1700s songbooks were a booming business. These were a special kind of songbook, with a condensed scale (the so-called *fasola* songbooks, as opposed to the "traditional" musical scale of *do-re-mi-fa-so-la-ti-do*) and with each note keyed to a particular shape, making them easy to follow for people without musical training. Schools were started to teach the new hymns, and by the turn of the century four-part harmony had made its timely appearance.

The camp meetings began in 1800 in Kentucky. To get a feeling for them, imagine a bluegrass music festival—part sacred, part picnic, part sheer entertainment. The Bible thumpers traveled across the South, preaching certain damnation and eternal fire with the spirit and flash of white James Browns. The crowd responded in kind, moaning and shouting with the preacher, suddenly breaking into spontaneous song that would eventually become ecstatic shouting. Sometimes they spoke in tongues or ritualistically handled snakes without fear (two activities still practiced in many places in the South). The music was simple, and, as black music, modified for the occasion. A song might come from a favorite drinking song or a hundred-year-old hymn, it made no difference—it was the singing, not the song, that was important.

The Great Revival, as it came to be known, spread from the South throughout the nation, sweeping the country into a religious fervor and, incidentally, spreading revivalist songs to every corner. For the first time white Americans found a way and a place to let go, to "act like a nigger" with impunity. They had a sanction to touch their senses, to discover their bodies, without risking eternal damnation and a whiff of the brimstone—and *that* was a lesson that white America would *never* forget!

Most importantly, the Great Revival gave white Americans their first taste of people's music, music that was to be experienced—lived—rather than appreciated at a distance. The music of the camp revivals made their grinding lives a bit more bearable—and thus the first brick was laid in the groundwork of "popular" music.

Ironically, as soon as that brick was laid, the powers that be set about to take the music away from the people. From roughly the Civil War on, the music was codified, cleaned up, and delivered unto the church choirs, who, as George Pullen Jackson has pointed out, began de-democratizing the music and rendering it passive rather than active. The old-time religion and its music hung on in a few scattered enclaves in the South, but for the most part a new kind of *gospel* music took root and grew among both blacks and whites, and both groups ultimately turned their backs on their "primitive" music.

Gospel music is the next building block of popular music, but, amazingly enough, it is the most segregated of the building blocks. There are actually two very distinct kinds of gospel, white and black. The reason for the separation is hard to understand, and the experts tend to gnaw around it. Since the 1930s both forms of gospel music have grown into huge national industries, selling millions of records a year and supporting literally hundreds of groups who make their living on the "gospel highway." In many cases, the blacks and whites sang the same songs, worshiped the same God, but were totally apart.

"It sounds trite," says William Ivey, the head of the prestigious Country Music Foundation in Nashville, Tennessee, and a student of gospel music, "but while there was always a certain amount of socializing between the races in popular music, in the sacred tradition the stereotyped rules of behavior seemed to be more strictly enforced."

At least for a while both sides of gospel music turned away from their roots, the simple music of the South, to the more conventional religious hymns, such as those by Isaac Watts, John Wesley, and the other popular authors of the Great Awakening. Part of the reason for this was the monumental inferiority complex that settled on the South at the close of the Civil War, a complex the South is only now beginning to shake off. From World War I on, South-baiting became something of a national mania. According to southern historian George Brown Tindall in his book *The Ethnic Southerner*, "a kind of neo-abolitionist myth of the Savage South was compounded. It seemed that the benighted South, after a period of relative neglect, suddenly became an object of concern to every publicist in the country."

Consider the anti-South crusade lead by H. L. Mencken in Baltimore. "Down there," Mencken wrote, "a poet is almost as rare as an oboe player, a dry-point etcher or a metaphysician." As for "critics, musical composers, painters, sculptors, architects . . . there is not even a bad one between the Potomac mud flats and the Gulf. Nor an historian. Nor a sociologist. Nor a philosopher. Nor a theologian. Nor a scientist. In all these fields the south is an awe-inspiring blank." He concluded one of his many attacks by calling the South "the Bible Belt," and the name stuck.

Not surprisingly, the old-time religion began to lay down its homespun hymnals and clean up its act. For the blacks, the situation was even more pressing. The total failure of Reconstruction and the subsequent exodus of blacks to the cities put increasing pressure on the "happy children" to grow up, and grow up fast, because the alternative was a lynch mob.

"Generally speaking, as far as religious music is concerned, there was a definite divergence between black
and white after the Civil War," said Dr. Samuel A. Floyd
of the Institute for Research in Black Music at Fisk University in Nashville. "The rise of 'Jim Crow' made interaction between the races rather impossible." Dr. Floyd
has identified three distinct trends in black religious music after the Civil War: a strong European choral tradition; the spirituals, which were already being altered
("European-ized") by whites; and the music of the black
Holiness and Pentecostal churches. That church music
would form the basis of what is now called black gospel
in a unique way. Although the songs sung were hymns,
their delivery was in the style we now call rhythm and
blues—"Amazing Grace" with soul, which would probably cause Dr. Isaac Watts to roll over in his grave (much
as rock would to Beethoven, one supposes).

At the same time, blacks gave birth to a secular music,
first the "rags," as picked on the piano by Scott Joplin,
then what would become the most important musical
forces in America, jazz and the blues. The blues especially were the opposite side of sacred—blues singers went
directly to hell, did not pass go, did not collect anything.
You could sing gospel or the blues, but never both. The
blues belonged to the Devil, with his high-rollin' ways
and high-yellow women, and if you sang his music, the
door to the Lord's house was shut to you. That's how it
was in 1905, and that's how it is today. Rufus Thomas, a
bluesman of long standing, the author of "The Dog" and
other classic soul hits of the 1960s for Stax Records in
Memphis, recently returned to the church to sing, and "I
have to tell you, I was scared to death, looking out there
at all those disapproving faces. But when I started sing-

ing, everybody accepted me." Then he decided to add a couple of gospel numbers to his stage show, along with "The Dog," "Does Your Monkey Do the Dog," and "The Funky Chicken." After the first show he was met backstage by a delegation of churchwomen, frowning. They could live with the fact that he sang "that music" for a living, the women told him, but it was immoral, unseemly, and probably illegal to include God's music and "that music" in the same show. He would have to stop it, and of course he did. "I remember standing there onstage while I was singing and wondering why people were walking out on me," he says, laughing, but not very loudly.

With the entrenchment of Jim Crow, the two gospel musics drifted further apart, unwilling to risk the interchange that was regularly going on in the honky-tonks and dives throughout the South. When W. C. Handy came to Beale Street in Memphis, Tennessee, in the early 1900s and began his ceaseless promotion of the blues, white folks began to pick up on the secular side of black music, until the blues and jazz far overshadowed gospel in popularity.

The result of the separate evolutions of the two gospel musics was, in the long run, earth-shattering. From the first white gospel music, which was deeply rooted in the Scotch-Irish ballad tradition of the Appalachian Mountains, came the string bands, the so-called old-time or hillbilly musicians. In the 1920s, while most of the country was shaking its collective body to *le jazz hot* and listening to the newly dominant radio, a sizable minority longed for a return to the good old days, when sin wasn't so overt. Canny radio and record men, sensing the build-

ing audience, dispatched missionaries to the mountains
to root out the string bands, record them, and turn their
music into a national craze. They succeeded beyond their
wildest imagination, and hillbilly music—renamed
"country" music for more genteel tastes—has grown into
one of the most powerful forces in modern music.

Black gospel singers, on the other hand, began honing
their sense of the beat, bringing blues rhythms and styl-
ings and a dynamic stage show to their performances.
Instrumental in this was Thomas A. Dorsey, a Georgian
who began his musical life as a blues singer called Georgia Tom (most famous for "It's Tight Like That"). In the
1930s, while the black quarters were already working the
gospel highway, Dorsey moved to Chicago and turned
away from the blues, at least in name. He never turned
away from the spirit of the blues, though, and pretty
soon his hymns were local legends. Some of those songs,
including "Precious Lord" and "Peace in the Valley,"
still stand as giants, taking their place among the great
religious songs of the ages. With Dorsey, gospel music
found the beat, and by the 1940s gospel was a moving
force in black music—such a moving force, in fact, that it
set the tone for black music well into the 1970s. In some
cases, the connection was overt—bluesman Bobby "Blue"
Bland worked with Ira Tucker, the head of the great gospel group the Dixie Hummingbirds (who later backed up
Paul Simon on his "Love Me Like a Rock" single).
Fledgling soul singer Sam Cooke sang lead with the Soul
Stirrers (the sexiest man in gospel music, he was called),
and it was there that he perfected a vocal style that
would influence Otis Redding, Al Green, and the other
great black singers of the next two decades. So many
black singers started singing in the church (including

Aretha Franklin, whose father, the Reverend C. L. Franklin, was a powerful voice in his own right; Marvin Gaye, whose father was also a minister; and even Otis Redding, who sang in church choirs before he became enamored of the style of Sam Cooke) that gospel is an omnipresent force, the music of Jesus playing peek-a-boo with blues, the music of the Devil, through every major trend of the last twenty years.

In the late 1940s and early 1950s the two gospel musics began touching again for the first time since the Civil War. Sparks flew, and from those sparks rock and roll was kindled.

WHAT HAPPENED
IN MEMPHIS

If you can believe the newspapers, they're going to make a shrine out of Graceland, the home of the fallen King of Rock and Roll. Everybody wants to buy Graceland, and from what I can make of the conflicting reports, whoever manages that feat will gold-plate the place and maybe erect a couple of statues besides. To make sure the world *really* knows what Memphis, Tennessee, thinks of its most famous resident.

A certain air of desperation surrounds all these goings on because Memphis—if you can boil a city of three-quarters of a million into a single word and have it mean anything—doesn't really know how it feels about Elvis Presley, even several long years after his death. To be sure, there's a tremendous amount of pressure on the city to "cash in" on the King—an Elvis Presley festival, maybe, along the lines of Nashville's tremendously successful Fan Fair, with a gold-plated Graceland as the

43

centerpiece. "Listen," I was told in Nashville by a heavy-weight in state government, "what in the hell is *wrong* with those people in Memphis? I mean, we've got country music here in Nashville, but they've got every other kind of music in the world in Memphis! They've got *Elvis*, f'god's sake! They've got a gold mine down there, and the more we talk to them, the more we're convinced that they're all crazy as loons! We're talking about making a fortune in tourism, and they're worried about whether black people like Elvis. Good Lord! If you know anybody down there who's playing with a full deck, *please* let me know!"

Memphis has a knack for generating that kind of histrionics—and the state official is not really as off base as he might seem at first view. In death, as in life, perhaps Elvis Presley belongs to us all. And maybe, Memphis is a little bit of hometown to all of us.

I grew up there, and I can feel the worry in the sticky summer air: What *are* we going to do about Elvis Presley? What possible memorial can we build (always said with a straight face) for a man who . . . who . . .

And there it is—a tiny hesitation, almost unnoticeable, immediately followed by an outpouring of praise for the King: He was the greatest; we're so proud of him; his music changed our lives; we *always* liked him, even when everybody was saying that he was just singing that . . . that . . .

See, he was always different, but he was always good to his family. Respectful—not at all like that crazy Jerry Lee Lewis. Did his time in the Army like a good boy should; didn't ask for any special favors or anything like that. Always said *yes-m'am* and *no-m'am;* gave to those less fortunate than himself; remembered the church; and

adored his mother. A good boy, and why would a good
boy want to sing . . . sing . . .

Nigger music.

And there it is, lying in wait like some old copperhead
under a rotted log.

Nigger music.

We are not talking here, as one fellow Memphian reminded me late one night in some nickel-and-dime
honky-tonk, about *good ole boys* singing *black* music. If
that's what I thought, then I was just wasting my time
and frying my brain in the heat for nothing at all.

"What *we are talking about* here is REDNECKS—the
meanest, lowest, gut-bustin'est, beer-drinkin'est, wife-
beatin'est *rednecks* in the whoooooooooooole wide world
singin' *nigger*—that's N-I-G-G-E-R—music!" my friend
said with a concluding sweep of the arm. "And *that* is
what happened in Memphis!"

In 1964 a black postman named Fred Hutchins paid
$3,500 to publish his own book, which he called *What
Happened in Memphis.* The slim red volume was filled with
stories he'd both witnessed and collected second-hand in
his forty years of walking the streets of Memphis deliver-
ing the mail, and before that working as a delivery man
for a Jewish stocking merchant who specialized in supplying silk stockings to whorehouses.

What intrigued Fred Hutchins was that what happened in Memphis was different from what happened in
most of the other places he was familiar with. Fate and
history had somehow conspired to push Memphis a few
degrees out of phase with the rest of the South, which
was, of course, totally askew from the rest of the country.
Memphis *was* different, in a way that was hard to put

your finger on. "Everybody there is crazy and they all speak in parables," said Jack Clement, once a producer for Sam Phillips at Sun Records in Memphis and now a firmly rooted Nashvillian.

What comes through most clearly in Hutchins' little book is the sense that Memphis *has* no history, that the series of events in the city's past don't hook together in any coherent order—as if the city was one of those alternate identities prepared for secret agents: the papers are all in order, a whole past created out of thin air, the only thing missing is a real person.

Memphis has no history, at least not one it wants to remember.

Some blame it on the fever, and they probably aren't too far from right. Yellow fever paid its fifth and most costly call on the slumbering city in 1878. When the first case was reported on August 13, Memphis was a booming city of fifty thousand people, an important river port and heir to the "new" South. Within eleven weeks it was a ghost town, with the only sound the creaking of the death wagons and the toneless call of that wagon's sole living passenger: "Bring out your dead . . . bring out your dead." In a panic to escape the fierce killer, twenty-five thousand people had fled the city—the rich, the landed gentry, the bankers, the merchants, the cotton and hardwood lords, everyone who could beg, borrow, or steal enough money to get out of town. Of those that remained, over five thousand died within those eleven weeks as all the cogs of the once bustling city ground to a halt. By the time the epidemic had run its course, grass was growing in the city's main street and the population had shrunk so much that the city charter was revoked. Quite simply, the city of Memphis had ceased to exist.

What grew up in its place bore only the slightest re-
semblance to the thriving old city. From across the South
people began making their way to Memphis—not the
rich, not the old-time southern aristocracy, but the plain-
dirt farmers, both black and white, the con men, the
gamblers, the rootless, the small merchants. They came
from as far away as the Carolinas and Virginia, some
taking the soon-to-be-legendary "Night Train to Memphis" in hopes of finding a better life there than they had
known on the farm. Blacks and whites were joined by the
common bond of the poor and by being strangers in a
strange land.

"The poor blacks and the poor whites were coming
together as early as 1900, playing music," said Judd Phillips, and Judd should know. In addition to being the
brother of Sam Phillips and the man who managed Jerry
Lee Lewis for years, Judd Phillips has an abiding love for
Memphis music and is one of the few people who have
made it a point to find out exactly how it came about.
"Within a hundred miles of Memphis—in the Delta—it
was strictly black, and at nights or on Sunday, when the
folks came in out of the fields, they'd get together in their
houses and play. Now, the white sharecroppers, who were
really working the same fields, would come around to
listen to them. The music was mostly guitar, sometimes
piano, maybe a trumpet, heavy on the bass beat. The
rhythm was syncopated, and in nearly every instance
they'd take a melody line from an old religious song and
adapt the lyric as befitted the times. Poor white trash and
poor black trash. You go a hundred miles east of here,
and you'll see a change in the houses—you'll see the big
plantation houses with the big slave shacks. You get
closer to Memphis, you see little sharecropper shacks. All

these elements, all these people, came together in this area, and you won't find it anyplace else in the world." Memphis, erased by a mosquito-borne virus, was rebuilt by an influx of plain and simple poor folks. The new society was at once more and less democratic than the old. While poverty put people on a more equal basis, the puritanical fundamentalist Christian churches ruled the day. And so Memphis began to develop a dual nature: a day side, whose community built churches like there was literally no tomorrow, condemned sinners, prized the Yankee work ethic, and tried to forget their plain-dirt beginnings; and a night side, which was a rip-roaring town to match anything the frontier West could dish up, with whorehouses and gambling, saloons on every street corner, rotgut liquor, marijuana, codeine, and cocaine for the asking. The opposing sides of the city simply ignored each other and went about their respective businesses.

Thomas Pinkston sat in his little house in south Memphis and remembered. What he remembered was another world, one that most Memphis citizens would like to forget entirely, or at the very least subject to a little judicious editing. He remembered Beale Street in its prime, the Home of the Blues, when rotgut whiskey flowed from a reputed 592 saloons and a man's life wasn't worth much more than a bullet in Mr. Colt's gun. He remembered the blues when they were young, and how they came to be.

"The blues started in them cotton fields," Tommy Pinkston said. "All you could do when the weather was dry was just sit there and see faraway places. Sing about them fields; sing about the Boss Man. Niggers hated their bosses, and they talked about them through song. If the Man be mean to you—now, I'm talking about what I heard; I'm talking about what I seen—you come into a saloon and sing your own song your own way."

Tommy Pinkston came to Beale Street before the 1920s, just in time to connect with one W. C. Handy, who happened to be a man who not only had an exceptional ear but could write music as well. Handy heard something in Memphis, and he set about to record it. For a while Tommy Pinkston played in his band, then Tommy began playing in the pit at the old Palace Theater. He played a song Mr. Handy had just written that extolled the virtues of a new politician named Ed Crump, who, according to the song, didn't allow any "easy riders" in Memphis.

Later the song was named "The Memphis Blues," but not before (some say) it delivered the black vote to Ed Crump, who wanted to be mayor of the born-again boom town of Memphis. Now if the honest truth be told, Mr. Crump not only allowed some easy riders around there, he did a little encouraging on the side. Folks called him "Boss" Crump, and he ran Memphis with an iron hand. He also ran Beale Street, which was not exactly part of Memphis.

Beale Street was a universe unto itself, the logical outgrowth of a city divided. Beale Street was the night side of Memphis, a black universe with its own natural laws (mostly thanks to Mr. Colt), its own government, its own rules and regulations, and more whorehouses per square inch than anyplace in America outside New Orleans' fabled Storyville. Something for everyone at every price— as long as the proper percentage found its way uptown to City Hall and the police department.

Outside of Memphis, they called it Murder U.S.A., the meanest street in America. It was said from the pulpit that the Devil himself lived on Beale Street, and the blues was his music.

IF BEALE STREET COULD TALK

The only difference between Memphis and Hell is that Memphis has a river running alongside of it, while Hell's river ran through it.
—A letter from a disgruntled tourist

The crumbling façade of Beale Street represents a major victory for the city of Memphis: the total elimination of an unruly black enclave, the killing of the blues. A Final Solution, American style.

Had it survived intact, Beale Street might have vied for the title of the Capital of Black America. Along with the honky-tonks and juke joints, Beale Street was also the home of a number of black professional men and women—doctors, dentists, accountants, photographers, and merchants. It was a major cultural center, and its wild and woolly ways drew people—from Richard Wright to James Baldwin to Martin Luther King—from across the country. And whatever else Beale Street was, it was

51

black, without shuffling, without apologies. A white man on Beale Street was an outsider, and that was, ultimately, intolerable.

The true story of the methodical destruction of Beale Street is hopelessly buried in bureaucratic paper shuffling and deals concluded with a handshake and a wink. Facts turn up like old cannonballs in a farmer's field—infrequently and unexpectedly. People in Memphis are uncomfortable with the ghosts that live on Beale Street and inhabit the lyrics to a thousand songs, and the reason they are uncomfortable goes back to my friend in that bar at the beginning of the last chapter. Memphis cannot become a city of brotherly love until it somehow finds a way to deal with the Question of Color. Even today Memphis remains obsessed with color. No sentence can be complete without the identification of all the proper adjectives. If you fail to insert that information in even the simplest of sentences, you can be sure you'll be asked for it.

"Beale Street was spontaneous," an editorial in the *Commercial Appeal,* the city's venerable morning daily paper, stated. "It was the absence of any kind of balance that made it.work."

Beale Street began its rise to fame during the Civil War, when the Union troops were headquartered there. Not surprisingly, Beale Street became a haven for the newly liberated blacks. As the yellow fever epidemics struck the city again and again, the overwhelming majority of the population that remained behind was black (in 1878 the ratio was two to one). By the turn of the century the indigenous black population was holding its own against the whites, whose big fashionable houses were pushing their way up Beale toward the river.

By that time Memphis had developed a Wild West reputation that made Tombstone, Arizona, seem civilized. Memphis became Murder U.S.A., the most dangerous place in the country. The *Commercial Appeal* called murder "the most thriving industry in Memphis" and pointed out that "They kill them next door to the city hall and they shoot them in the parks."

The situation was so bad by 1906 that an old black woman with a reputation as a seer predicted that God had had enough of Sodom-on-the-Mississippi, and that on Tuesday, March 27, 1906, Memphis would sink into a huge hole for its sins. She also promised two days of gloom before the earth swallowed the city, and, as such things are wont, March 25 and 26 were gloomy indeed, prompting thousands of Memphians to get out of town quickly.

Memphis made it safely through the 27th of March with little more than a thunderstorm, but the city hardly took the reprieve seriously. Blacks were especially hard hit—at a meeting of citizens concerned over the nightly carnage one civil leader called for an end to the killing of Negroes by white men, since there was a clear danger that this could lead to the killing of white men.

If the beginnings of the Home of the Blues were inauspicious, its endings were even more so. The rumblings demanding a "fixing" of Beale Street began around 1959 (although diehard old-timers usually place the date closer to 1941, when the city closed the whorehouses). The late 1950s saw a flurry of interest in Beale Street on two fronts: how to get rid of it, and how to make money off it at the same time. In 1959 then-Mayor Edmund Orgill called for turning Beale Street into "Memphis's Bourbon Street," a theme that was repeated throughout the next decade. The following year W. C. Handy Park, a tiny snatch of greenery across from the Pantaze Drug Store and Club Handy, was dedicated, leading many people to believe that a New Orleans-style revitalization was just around the corner.

Actually, revitalization was hardly what was wanted; the main problem was all the Negroes who insisted on making Beale Street their home.

What "normal family" in their right mind, the reasoning went, was going to go down to Handy Park for a little culture and risk being carved up by some "person" wearing an electric orange suit and running a string of girls on the side? In New Orleans people could go down to Bourbon Street without worrying about waking up dead the next morning. *White* people could listen to *black* music there with impunity. And, after all, how could you learn to appreciate something if while you were listening, you were scared out of your wits? Clearly something had to be done about the "Beale Street problem."

The first step was to declare Beale Street dead, which was absolutely not the case. Undeniably, the street had seen better days, but business was still flourishing in the 1960s, and you could still hear just about any music you wanted to along Beale's sidewalks. The secret of Beale Street was, in fact, that nothing—except people—ever seemed to die there. People across the country may have temporarily forgotten the blues, but they were there for the asking on Beale Street. Bands were still playing swing and the jazz was still hot; the musical cauldron was still bubbling, a dark black brew with a dash of white thrown in every now and then. It was still a different world, a black world that refused to pay even lip service to the idea of integration. On Beale Street the key word was survival.

When Dr. Martin Luther King was killed within spitting distance of Beale in 1968, there were 625 buildings
standing along Beale. Today there are fewer than 65. The
shot that ended a life at the Lorraine Motel also tolled
the death of Beale Street. The ensuing violence, even
in an area where violence was far from rare, was the
"proof" that the "Beale Street problem" had to be dealt
with fast. Within a year the housing authority began
bulldozing the slums for blocks and blocks around Beale
Street, in ironic imitation of the American strategy in
Vietnam. Deny the enemy a home; destroy the villages;
cut him off from his roots. With his ties severed, the enemy will wither and die, his kin will scatter and resettle.
The policy that failed so miserably in Southeast Asia
worked spectacularly in Memphis. Suddenly the people
who made Beale Street perk found they had no home.
Bluesmen who had spent forty years of their lives along
Beale Street were resettled in different areas of town,
away from the clubs, the honky-tonks, the other musicians. The restaurants had no business; the pawn shops'
walk-in trade began running down like an old broken
clock. People didn't much like to take a special trip
across town to see a show or go to a movie.

Beale Street began to die.

The city continued its relentless urban renewal plan.
Under the threat of condemnation, businesses were
forced to sell out to the city and leave Beale Street. Once
the city owned the buildings, they were literally left to
rot, the wind, rain, rats, derelicts, and fires gnawing at
their guts. While there was much public hand wringing
over the "sad state" of Beale Street, nothing was done to
reverse or even stem the deterioration. Finally the city
decided to make Beale safe for the few pedestrians who
made their way there by condemning the whole lot of

buildings, bulldozing them flat, and then building something in the spirit of old Beale Street, but tasteful.

Oh, there were plenty of rationalizations. I worked for the city government at the time, and I heard them all. What they boiled down to was this: We've got the power, and we can do what we want. Period. Beale Street was razed except for a four-block segment listed with the National Register of Historic Places. That, too, would have been ground down had not the federal government frowned on the bulldozing of historical landmarks.

"This city has spent 26 million dollars over the past twenty years to create the look of Hiroshima in 1946," said Memphis State University historian Dr. F. Jack Hurley about the renovation of Beale Street. "Only in Hiroshima, we did it a lot quicker."

That is how Beale Street was prepared to become the Disneyland of the Blues, safe for people of all ages, races, colors, and creeds. At this point $5.5 million is earmarked for the reconstruction of Beale Street, and eight federal and ten local agencies are involved in the "resurrection." If you want to rent one of the crumbling hulks along the street, be prepared to try and make heads or tails of a sixty-six-page lease and to fork over a whole lot of money—the buildings are literally falling down and physical renovation will be expensive. So far there have been six "comprehensive" studies made of the Beale Street problem, and no doubt there'll be many more before the city of Memphis regrets what it tore down.

If Beale Street could talk, wrote Handy, if Beale Street could talk . . . One gets the eerie feeling walking down the sad street that it wants to talk very badly, that each building is trying to push aside the plywood and the rot and say something very important, if only we could hear the words.

When the Memphis Development Foundation, one of the many groups trying to organize the "Beale Street Project" (which is what the "Beale Street problem" has become), decided to make a record album about Beale Street to boost their cause, they turned, perhaps fittingly, not to one of the street's black regulars, but to a white named James Luther Dickinson. Dickinson's credits were impressive—he had toured with the Rolling Stones as a keyboard man, worked with the seminal Dixie Flyers in Miami, and produced extensively, including working for Ry Cooder.

The results were spectacular, if unexpected. The album, *Beale Street Saturday Night,* is a masterpiece, going beyond the idea of a record to become, as one writer called it, a folk tale, a tiny mirror of Beale Street the way it was. The song was sung by Sid Selvidge, another white, and he melded perfectly with such Beale Street greats as Furry Lewis and Sleepy John Estes and Prince Gabe.

Proving, perhaps, that some people can still hear the words.

AN INTERLUDE ON BEALE STREET

Sometimes the blues made themselves felt in the oddest of ways, as exemplified by this story told to me by a man who owned a dance studio on Beale Street in the mid-1920s. Even today he breaks into a sweat when recounting it.

The dance teacher is preening in front of a mirror. He is good and he knows it, and he strikes a handsome figure. He is so good that even some of the white dance studios that have sprung up like mushrooms after a summer rain have invited him and some of his professional dancers to perform at their studios, giving blacks and whites a chance to swap steps. His own studio, on Beale Street of course, has a balcony, where white dancers can come to watch the sweating black bodies work out and learn, if they can, the intricate, flashy dances of the mean streets.

The dance teacher returns to his job, which for this night is head waiter at a swank country club about ten blocks from Beale. He is especially pleased on this particular night because he is well on his way to becoming something of a celebrity. He has invented a dance, which he has named the Cootie Crawl, and it is sweeping Beale Street like fire through a tenement. The dance is fast and frantic, with the music built around the dance steps by a musician who used to be in Mr. Handy's band. *Everyone* is dancing the Cootie Crawl, and the dance teacher can't help but smile at the notion.

While he is smiling he is approached by a young white couple in their late teens or early twenties. When the couple introduce themselves, he realizes that he's heard of them. Dancing has swept the country, and a local theater—part of a national chain of dance ballrooms—has sponsored a contest. This young couple were the winners.

They will tour the country, dancing at every ballroom in the chain, and if the fates are kind, they will dance their way to fame and fortune in Hollywood. At least that's how it's written in the pulps, and the dance teacher's eyes harden at the thought of it. What they want from the dance teacher, after much hemming and hawing, is to learn the Cootie Crawl for their dance routine, to carry the craze from darkest Beale Street to whitest America.

The dance teacher is at once flattered and irritated.

Maybe, he reminds the young couple, they've forgotten how it is. White and black don't mix. The dance teacher is haughty, but the young couple are persuasive—it is, after all, the Jazz Age. The world, as everyone knows, is in a tear.

Okay, the dance teacher agrees. Be at my studio on Beale Street tomorrow evening. The couple are ecstatic. There is, however, one condition. "You," he says to the girl, "have to bring your parents. I don't want no trouble. You watch me and my partner and maybe pick up the Cootie Crawl that way."

The couple move away, muttering their thanks. There is, the dance teacher thinks, just no figuring white folks.

The appointed day arrives, and the dance teacher has the studio set up just so. Still, he is nervous when the couple finally arrive, the girl with her mother in tow. He shows them around the studio, stalling, then finally announces that he's going across the street to get his dance partner, who's stopped off for a bite to eat.

How much, the mother ventures, is the lesson going to cost?

"Fifty dollars," says the dance teacher smugly. Fifty dollars is a lot of money in 1925.

"Fifty dollars will be just fine," the mother says.

"What I meant was fifty dollars for me and fifty dollars for my partner," says the dance teacher. If she's that quick with fifty, she's probably that quick with a hundred.

"Fifty for each is just fine," she says, nonplused.

The dance teacher smiles and makes a quick exit, crossing Beale Street to the dive where his partner is sipping a shot of fake whiskey. It's all set up, he says. Fifty dollars apiece, so come on.

She is more than a little bleary, and she's not having any part of it. "Listen," she tells the dance teacher, "you go tell those white peckerwoods that I don't *feel* like teaching them to dance!"

"You're crazy!" he snaps. "We're talkin' about fifty dollars and where else can you get that kind of money without being on your back!"

"I don't give a damn what it is!" she shouts, and the bar patrons turn to watch. "I'm not going to dance for no white folks!"

The dance teacher shrugs and leaves the bar, crossing the street and reentering his studio. Very sorry, he tells his clients, but my partner has been taken unexpectedly ill, and there'll be no lesson tonight.

"Didn't you teach your partner the dance?" says the young white girl.

The dance teacher nods yes, questioningly.

"Then you can teach me."

The dance teacher feels sweat break out on his brow and under his arms. The mother is smiling; the girl's dance partner is studiously staring at the wall. The girl is looking straight at him, and the dance teacher can't help but notice that she is pretty, and that she is saucy. And that spells trouble, big trouble.

Perhaps, he says diplomatically, you don't understand how the dance is done. There is, ah, quite a lot of *embracing,* if you get my meaning. A lot of *touching,* if you understand me. "Under the circumstances, I don't see how I could personally teach you the dance."

In his head the dance teacher sees the headlines— "Negro Boy Assaults White Woman . . . Said It Was Supposed to Be a Dance." He imagines the breaking of glass as a brick flies through the window of his home, hears the shouts as the crowd gathers in his mind . . . "You touched a white woman, nigger! You gonna pay for that touch, nigger!" The girl's eyes are gleaming and her lips are parted, ever so slightly. It is 1925, and these are heady times. Very heady times.

The mother smiles beatifically. "That's all right," she says. "Whatever you have to do to teach her the dance, do so. It's perfectly all right." The male dance partner says nothing, but he is looking at the girl, and maybe he is breathing a speck harder.

The dance teacher is beginning to panic. It was only a few years ago, in 1917, that a black man was charged in the rape and mutilation of a sixteen-year-old white girl, not much younger than the girl the dance teacher is facing at this moment. They'd turned that black man over to the crowds, since the police figured lynching was too good for him. The crowd built a big fire with the black man as the main log, and when it was over, they cut off his head and rolled it down Beale Street. There wasn't any evidence in that case, either. The dance teacher tries one more time:

"See, the main step is a dip, and we go down almost to a squat," the dance teacher says. "Then our legs . . . well, our legs will be between each other's, and that's when we Cootie Crawl. I mean, we embrace, uh, tightly, and then we come up together, all the way, embracing. That's the way it's got to be. That's the dance . . ."

"That's all right," the mother says. The girl is smiling, looking impatient. Her breasts aren't bound, the dance teacher notices against his will, and her nipples are hard.

The girl and her mother smile, the dance partner alternately stares at the wall and at his partner, the dance teacher says nothing. Nothing, he thinks, good can come of this, but he is outvoted.

"Okay," he says, "I'll teach you my dance."

It takes twenty minutes. She is wearing a dress, and his leg pushes it above her knee to the very top of her stockings. Her own leg is skating along his thigh, making no effort to conceal its presence in his groin. The dance teacher is alternately aroused and terrified. His pupil is quite obviously only the former. When they embrace, he barely touches her back, but she pulls him close, until he can feel her nipples against his chest. She is smiling and she is brazen. Her dance partner is leering unabashedly as his girl slowly rides up and down with the dance teacher, watching her legs slide in and out of her dress. The mother is smiling, as if she were visiting a library luncheon. It is, after all, the Jazz Age, and all things are possible.

The dance teacher is covered with sweat, and visions of brickbats and ropes alternate with images of the white girl in his arms. Twenty minutes, thirty minutes, then he gestures to her dance partner—"Now you try."

The atmosphere in the room is instantly lighter, and a semblance of normalcy returns. Pretty soon the partner has it down pat, and they prepare to leave. The dance teacher pockets the hundred bucks and shows them to the door, where he sees the black crowds moving up and down Beale Street. He breathes in the murky air like a condemned man who's just received a pardon. You must come to dinner, the mother insists, and later he does. He goes in the front door and sits at the table with the other people, all white, and the dance teacher is uncomfortable, even if it *is* the Jazz Age. Later the girl dances the Cootie Crawl across the country and goes on to Hollywood, where she does indeed become somewhat famous. She sends the dance teacher postcards, and later letters, but when they come, he just throws them away. First he tears them up into little pieces, then he remembers touching her, then he throws the letters away.

Later the Jazz Age ends.

THE TALKIN'
BEALE STREET BLUES

Without oppression and without racism, you have no blues.
> —*Toward the African Revolution*
> by Frantz Fanon

You ain't talkin' about what you know. You ain't talkin' about the blues, 'cause you don't know the blues.
> —Tommy Pinkston

A thick chunk of ham sizzles in the big cast-iron skillet and Lillie Mae Glover—also known as Memphis Ma Rainey—is busily slicing thick slabs of a fresh tomato. "Lawdy me, boy!" she says while I cower on the over-stuffed couch. "You look like you're starving to death, and nobody's gonna starve to death while Ma Rainey can still handle a skillet!"

The apartment is a second-floor walkup on Lauderdale, a couple of miles from the wreckage of Beale Street.

The walls are gray-green, and the main window looks out over the neighborhood ("Lawd, don't they mind everybody else's business but their own!"). On the walls are two religious tapestries and a number of yellow Sun Records from her brief recording career with Sam Phillips. At sixty-eight years of age and a "tiny" 250 pounds, Ma Rainey has enough spare energy to shame me into silence. She is effervescent and unnerving, wielding the huge skillet like a pencil to make her point. No amount of begging off will do—an emaciated white boy has come to her door, and a touch of the grandmother in her soul won't allow him to leave unsatisfied.

"Lawd!"—she prefaces everything with "Lawd!", a brief prayer to expiate her sins of the flesh—"You just sit right there and let Ma Rainey tell you about the blues. We'll get some food in you, and we'll talk about the blues!"

Eventually I am facing a ham sandwich about three inches thick with grease and tomato juice rapidly dissolving the bread, and, true to her word, she talks about the blues.

"I've always been a show stopper," she says, "and I guess that's because I put my whole heart into it. I always put my whole heart into it. I am the black sheep of my family, though. There was thirteen of us, and all of them wanted to be something 'cept me. I wanted to be a blues singer."

She rears back and laughs, and the sheer joy of that laughter fills the kitchen and bubbles out onto the streets.

"The blues, I guess they were born in me," she says, plopping her weight on a painfully abused kitchen stool. "I guess I slipped off when I was nine or ten—we lived in Nashville then—to a medicine show, and I got up there on the little stage and I started singing the blues. Well, my mamma caught me and she beat me all the way home. Lawd, she beat me! My daddy was a preacher in a sanctified church, and he wouldn't have no blues singing in his house."

The beating gave her hapless parents a few years' respite until a man named Tom Simpson happened along. Fourteen-year-old Lillie Mae knew she was in love and didn't waste any time. She and Tom ran away to join a carnival show, and she started singing the blues for real. Not too surprisingly, the blues proved to be both a better provider and a better friend than Tom Simpson, and pretty soon she was on her own, traveling around the country in a procession of minstrel shows.

"We'd go to places where they'd never seen a colored person before. I remember once in Illinois, when we rolled into this little town, they thought we was no-tailed bears! Lawd, can you believe that? No-tailed bears!" She roars with laughter. "Can you believe I slept in a trunk and weighed 135 pounds? I tell you, I was a li'l ole fast girl."

In her travels she met and performed with the very biggest stars—Bessie Smith, Ida Cox, and Ma Rainey, whose place Little Mae would take when the original Ma Rainey couldn't go on. Pretty soon she was known as Baby Ma Rainey, and she kept that name right up until 1928, when she found Beale Street and realized she was home. For a while, she even joined the chorus, playing at the bigger theaters on Beale. But she got a hankering to be out front again; she wanted to be the person who opened the show, a comedienne. After much badgering and harassment (and—the implication is clear—the heavy application of feminine wiles) Lillie Mae got her shot.

She made herself a pair of gingham coveralls, got a white cap and some white tennis shoes, blacked one tooth, and, after much practice in front of the mirror, went on to "open the oleo"—in blackface.

"I walked out on that stage and I said, 'Hold it! Don't do nothing till you hear from me!' They didn't know whether I was a boy or a girl, and pretty soon I was a regular. I didn't do nothing but open the oleo and sing the blues, honey!"

The minstrel tradition remained strong—blacks now appeared in blackface, as whites had once done in imitation of blacks. Gus Cannon, one of the greatest bluesmen to ever make his home in Memphis, recalled that once his face was corked and his mouth was painted white, he had to take a shot of whiskey before he could go on stage. It was hard, he said, to be funny to those people.

But times got harder on Beale Street: the Depression came, then the war, and the days when you could go down the streets with a dime and win yourself three or four hundred dollars at craps were over for good. "Memphis" Ma Rainey kept right on singing the blues for anybody who would listen, and for a while she "rented rooms" for a little extra money. The rooms were rented to girls for an hour or however long business would take, and on a good night she could clear two or three hundred dollars. But even that business dried up, and plain old Lillie Mae Glover found herself working at the Firestone factory, making tires.

The story might have gone on to its predictable unhappy ending had it not been for Harry Godwin, a local white promoter, manager, and what-have-you with an abiding love for the blues *and* the people who sang them.

"Mr. Godwin heard I was sick and he came to see me,"

she says, rocking back and forth on her precarious perch. "I was in bad shape. I couldn't work . . . I just couldn't do nothing. And Mr. Godwin says, 'I'm going to take you to a club. You don't have to sing, but you need to get out of the house.' So we got there, and he tricked me into singing a number, and then everybody was applauding and coming up to me and asking how I was, if I was going to sing there again. And I just got disgusted with myself. I knew that I was born to sing the blues, and I wouldn't be all right until I was singing the blues again. And now I'm all right."

And indeed she is. It is years since I first saw her and she is still singing the blues. She is a star at a club called Blues Alley, the very first blues club in Memphis in a couple of decades. The kids come, they love all 250 pounds of her, and she accepts the applause like a queen. If there is someone who watches over fools and blues singers, then I think we owe him some thanks for this happy ending, because on Beale Street, such endings are few and far between.

More than any other form of music, the blues are an academician's delight. They are just alien enough to supply that thrill of plunging into the unknown without actually having to hack through jungle vines with a machete; and just recent enough that the original practitioners can be dredged up for information. And, as Paul Oliver points out in his landmark work on the music, *The Story of the Blues,* the blues may be the last great folk music the Western world will produce. Folk music—that is, the music of shared aspirations, beliefs, and desires by one particular group of people—requires isolation in which to germinate and grow. For all intents and purposes, that isolation no longer exists. We are a society shaped by our mass media, and there doesn't seem to be a medium that *isn't* mass. Like the natives of Panama whose native craft, a strange kind of reverse quilting in which layers and layers of brightly colored material are stitched together to form a pattern, called a *mola*, now includes images of rocket ships, Coca-Cola cans, and cars, we have become part of Marshall McLuhan's much vaunted Global Village, and our culture—especially our music—is being run through a blender.

The blues, though, are something organic, as much a part of the natural cycle as the changing of the seasons. When it came time for the blues to appear, they blossomed all over the South, from the cotton fields of the Mississippi Delta to the back streets of Atlanta and Tampa. The early blues songs were the flip side of black gospel music, which preached transcendence of the day-to-day world in return for acceptance in the Great By-and-By. What the blues said was that tomorrow might be worse; but if tomorrow couldn't be depended on, you knew what you had today. Take it while you can get it, and leave the Great By-and-By to take care of itself.

The blues refused to follow any one particular pattern. They could be the dim, nightmarish visions of Robert Johnson, whose brief life was marked by a hell hound on his trail and whose dark visions of a world out of kilter inspired the work of the Rolling Stones, Eric Clapton, and many others; or the ribald ramblings of Furry Lewis, whose greatest concern seemed to be where the next woman was coming from ("Why," he bragged once, "should I bother getting a wife when the man next door got one just as good?").

More than a music, the blues are a feeling, a way of

making sense of a universe that at times seems as crazy as a drunken duck. They grew out of the old field hollers of the slaves and were tempered by black gospel and the "rags" from turn-of-the-century minstrel shows.

It's impossible to date precisely when the blues arrived on Beale Street. W. C. Handy first heard the form in 1903 at a railroad station in Tutwiler, Mississippi, and by the time he arrived in Memphis a few years later, the blues were firmly entrenched all along the street. Whenever the blues arrived, though, they came as a country cousin into a rip-roaring town, and to survive, they had to learn the ways of the street. Obligingly, cottonpatch blues began to mix with big-band music and the more uptempo dance music that came to be called the jump blues. There was a jazz influence and even a touch of hillbilly— Memphis Ma Rainey remembers that some of her most requested numbers in those Beale Street watering holes were hillbilly songs popular at the time. In the cauldron of Beale Street the blues found their most endearing home and, ultimately, their greatest influence. The old country blues players worked the street (where W. C. Handy found much of his material), and the bands played the clubs, but it was not at all unusual to see the boys in the band out on the street, picking up the licks. For a band to stay alive in the heyday of Beale Street, it had to be able to play anything, from straight blues to Benny Goodman stuff, from rocking rhythm and blues to jazz.

"If you were a musician on Beale Street, everything was okay for you," said Dub Jenkins, the leader of one of the best of the Beale Street bands. "The rough guys kept things in line, and the police kept away. We were playing jazz, rhythm and blues, Duke Ellington stuff, swing like

Benny Goodman, even some blues, because the people liked it."

If your baby had gone and you were down to your last dime, and couldn't afford a shot of even the bootleg stuff—in other words, if you *really* wanted to hear some blues—the place to go was the gambling joints, the crap houses. There the blues ruled supreme, and your last dime could lead to either a fortune or a quick death. That is the Beale Street that Thomas Pinkston remembers so well.

The first time I met Tommy Pinkston was at the invitation of a mutual white friend who was worried that Tommy might throw me out because of the color of my skin. "He's not real fond of white people," the friend cautioned, "and I can't really say as I blame him."

Together we made the trek to south Memphis, to a modest white house in a modest neighborhood that was holding its own against the creeping blight only a few blocks away. The door had an ornamental iron screen that could do double duty at a bank, but the old man behind the door was spry and more than a little suspicious. Introductions were made, and the mutual friend exited, leaving me to tread water on my own.

"Whatever you do with what I tell you, I guess you're going to make some money off it, ain't you?" asked Tommy Pinkston. He wasn't really asking a question but stating a painfully obvious fact: Here's another white boy come around to take what he can and split. I'll be damned if he wasn't absolutely right.

"I make a little money," I said. Normally I avoid liberal guilt like the plague.

"And I don't," he said.

"We do," I said rather stupidly, "what we can."

His eyes locked with mine, and he held the stare for a long time, then he shrugged his shoulders. When the chips are down, the white boy always wins.

"Before you were born," Tommy Pinkston said, "Beale Street wasn't nothing but pawn shops, policy houses, and houses of prostitution. You don't know that, 'cause you weren't even born. I was there. I'll tell you what I saw. This is the blues I'm talking about, and you listen."

And listen I did, because in all of Memphis there is probably no greater body of knowledge about how it really was on Beale Street than Tommy Pinkston, second fiddle in Handy's band, pit player at the old Palace Theater. He came to Beale Street as a young man before World War I, his true age lost in the casual record-keeping of the old century. He was something of a musical prodigy and fell under the tutelage of one Joe Cortese, a white man who arranged for Pinkston to attend the all-white Memphis Music School to learn the violin.

Pinkston's cousin had been a field hand, a bluesman of the old tradition, and his mother had run away from home to live with a white man. "In those times a white man always had to get himself a colored girl," he says. "And my mama, she didn't have anything to do with the other coloreds. She was whiter than you—this is a fact." When the family moved to Memphis in 1915, Pinkston's aunt ran a flophouse restaurant off Beale, where W. C. Handy regularly dropped by for the fifteen-cent special—black-eyed peas and sweet potatoes. Handy took a shine to the young violin player, and pretty soon Pinkston was playing all night at the honky-tonks with Handy's band, "for the experience, see. Some nights, the whole band only got three dollars for playing, and Mr. Handy finally got disgusted and went to New York City."

Handy's loss was Beale Street's gain. For the next five years Pinkston played in the pit of the Palace Theater as part of the house band that backed the greatest of the blues immortals—Bessie Smith, Ida Cox, Memphis Minnie, Bessie Brown, Count Basie, Duke Ellington, Jelly Roll Morton. "I knew 'em all, and they were my friends. Bessie Smith was the greatest who ever done it, who sang the blues. That's the truth. Diana Ross don't know nothing about singing the blues. That's the truth."

Perhaps more importantly, Tommy Pinkston soaked up the lore of Beale Street like a sponge. He moved easily among the street people, listening to their stories and joining in their diversions. He took an equal amount of interest in the musical theories of the big bands and the doings of mulatto prostitutes, and through it all he began to develop a fierce pride in his race. It went beyond what would become known as "Black Power" almost half a century later. What Tommy Pinkston took pride in was *strength*, the strength that kept the black race alive and together against literally incredible odds. "Mr. Handy used to tell me this back fifty years ago," Tommy Pinkston later told Jim Dickinson for the *Beale Street Saturday Night* album. "I'll tell you what he told me. I don't care what the people say about this country—you can't beat it. This is the greatest place on earth, the United States of America. . . . My grandmother was a full-blooded African . . . and she landed in Mobile, Alabama. I don't know what part of Africa she was from. But I'm gonna tell ya'll something. I don't care what I say. The American white man and the American Negro are the most advanced two figures on earth. Nobody can outdo us. They can't whip us. Nobody. Just suppose I'd been over

in Africa, sitting up in a banana tree now with that di-
aper on eatin' a banana and hollering 'Boola-boola!' I'm
glad they brought me here! It helped.''

Tommy Pinkston saw strength and dignity in the
lowest crapshooter, and within the confines of his own
culture—a confinement that we can hardly even *imagine*
today—fashioned that strength and dignity into a statement of faith in what it meant to be black. That statement echoes down through the years in the most unlikely
places, from Dr. Martin Luther King, who, like W. C.
Handy, shared an abiding belief in America and its peoples and who died within sight of Beale Street, to Curtis
Mayfield, who looked to the street and found his statement in a black cocaine dealer named Superfly.

Interestingly enough, the great upsurge in black consciousness in the 1950s and 1960s—an upsurge that saw
the emergence of many black arts and crafts and traditions for the first time into widespread public view—refused to acknowledge the blues. Instead, original African
music had its brief time in the sun, followed by an interest in early jazz.

The reasons are both very simple and very complicated. At the top of the simple list is a reason that's in-
grained in our subconscious—the younger generation
rejects the values and traditions of the older generation,
particularly if that older generation is thought of as
"country cousins." The blues also suffered from a radical
analysis expressed by Frantz Fanon, one of the best-
known radical philosophers of the 1960s. "Thus the
Blues—the Black slave lament—was offered up for the admiration of the oppressors," he wrote in *Toward the African
Revolution* in 1967. "This modicum of stylized oppression
is the exploiter's and the racist's rightful due. Without

oppression and without racism you have no blues. The end of racism would sound the knell of great Negro music. . . ."

The complaint was that the blues weren't *pure;* they carried the irrevocable taint of the plantations. Further, the blues were and are earthy music, more concerned with the day-to-day victories and defeats of a single man than with sweeping vistas of social change.

"If the Man be mean to you," said Tommy Pinkston, "and I've seen this; I'm not talking about what I've heard—then you go into a saloon and sing your own song your own way, and that was the blues. People would run you out of their place when you started playing the blues, 'cause they didn't like it. The blues came out of those cotton fields. All you could do when the weather was dry, all you could do was sit and see faraway places in your head. That was the blues."

His eyes were electric, and from his living room on Hamilton Street Tommy Pinkston saw places far away in time and space. "On days like today, we'd go way back in the country and make us a billy-goat wagon, my brother and I did. These boys would be there, and they'd play the Jew's harp, and some of them would dance and sing. We'd sing about girls. They'd sing about their boss, who was a white man, and sometimes he was mean and sometimes he ain't. That's the blues. Sometimes we'd catch a young steer and we'd ride him around, and I remember that the girls out in the country then used to put hot rags on their heads to straighten their hair. That's true, what I'm tellin' you. That's the blues."

Defining the blues is, ultimately, like defining the hot wind that stirs up dust devils in dry cotton patches. Like the wind, the blues simply exist. Academicians—especially white academicians—routinely comment that it is a shame the blues didn't address themselves to the overwhelming black problems of the time; that one of the reasons for the music's lack of acceptance was this failure. (The very few blues songs that did deal with such concerns have been documented wildly out of proportion to their influence.)

Simply put, the blues were the music of survival, the songs of troubled men in troubled times. Their message was that life was transitory, pleasures few, and dangers many. They said, "Be strong and enjoy while you can," and a more revolutionary message can hardly be imagined. The blues were people's music, and it is not surprising that the most influential music of any generation has always been people's music. Blues, rhythm and blues, early rock, southern rock, even country music, none embraced the pretension best expressed in a latter-day rock song, thinking it could change the world . . .

People's music says just the opposite: No, we *cannot* change the world. The best we can hope for is to survive; and if we are lucky, we can change ourselves.

That's the blues.

"Anytime someone wants to call me 'nigger,' I give him the privilege, because only a Nigger could have subdued and gone through the things that we, the Black people, have gone through and survived," bluesman Johnny Shines told interviewers Robert Neff and Anthony Conner in 1975. "So if you call me 'nigger,' you only identify me as one of the strongest in the world. I feel like it's an honor, not a disgrace, to be called 'nigger.' To me it tells me I am the strongest. Only me and a beast of burden—such as an ox—could have subdued and survived. Anything else would have been extinct by now."

"Then there was Zack Slack, he played piano in a whorehouse; Ready Money, the oldest prostitute on Beale Street—we called her that 'cause she could always get ready money; Little Ona, the best pickpocket in the whole United States; Gorilla Jones, a prizefighter and a bootlegger who used to work with Machine Gun Kelly next to the Palace Theater." Tommy Pinkston was reliving a world gone to dust, bright-painted plywood windows for its tombstone. "Annie Mitchell, Mirror Hood, they were beautiful girls, colored girls, but they only went with white men. The nigger girls were cheap—anybody could buy it cheap. Just off Beale, on Gayoso, they had the houses, but they were for whites only. Black girls and mulattos, but coloreds weren't allowed in.

"Thursday night we had what we called the Midnite Ramble at the Palace, and that's when the white people would come down to Beale Street and listen to the music. I used to watch 'em, and I seen 'em out there, taking notes while we was playing. I saw them out there, stealin' our music."

Since that first meeting Tommy Pinkston has mellowed a bit, returning to play a few concerts to "show you young kids what real music is" and talking about Beale Street to the respectful, mostly white folks who come to listen. He remembers what he's seen, and he remembers what he's been told. He tells the story of how Ben Griffin was killed at the Monarch, and with each telling the story gets better and better. He tells the story of Wild Bill Latura, who on the evening of December 10, 1908, walked into Hammet Ashford's saloon and gambling establishment and shot seven people with his .38, being something of a sore loser at the crap tables. When the police arrested him and hauled him into court, Wild

Bill's statement was short and to the point: "I just shot 'em and that's all there is to it." The story goes that Wild Bill was enraged beyond thinking because a young reporter in the *Commercial Appeal* referred to him as one of the city's biggest tourist attractions. He was acquitted—he was white—but eventually he met his doom from a police revolver.

"Beale Street was the greatest place in the world until they ruint it," says Tommy Pinkston.

Listen to him. That's the blues.

WHITE MAN'S BLUES

Most folk songs are like jokes; everybody knows them, but nobody knows who invented them.

—*Blacks, Whites, and Blues*
by Tony Russell

Like some caricature of a country queen, the long blond hair of country music has always had its short black roots, and, oddly enough, most country musicians have never forgotten those roots. More than any other musical form, country music has retained its close connection with black music, even though the two audiences have remained totally separate—or so it seemed.

As Frye Gaillard wrote in *Watermelon Wine: The Spirit of Country Music,* "Even in the years of peak segregation, the separation was never as complete as the mythology insisted it was." While the two churches remained aloof, white country musicians found themselves irresistibly drawn to the music of the black honky-tonks and street singers, and from the very beginnings of country music that black influence has played a significant role in the music called "white man's blues."

Part of the connection was overt—most of the older country singers learned their craft from two sources, the Grand Ole Opry on the radio and a black mentor nearby. Jimmie Rodgers, Hank Williams, Charlie Rich, Conway Twitty, Merle Travis, Chet Atkins, and dozens of others first learned the blues at the knees of obscure field hands and street singers. The remainder of the connection, though, is more nebulous. Country music and black music, especially the blues, grew up together, sharing the same landscape, the same economic stratum (poor and rural), the same trials and tribulations. "Consider the landscape," wrote Tony Russell in *Blacks, Whites and Blues*. "A musician would be open to sounds from every direction; from family and friends, from field and railroad yard, lumber camp and mine; from street singers and traveling show musicians; from phonograph records and radio; from dances and suppers and camp-meetings and carnivals; from fellow prisoners in jails, from fellow workmen everywhere. A white youngster could learn a song or a tune not only in the bosom of his family but from their black employees—mammy, Uncle Remus or anyone else."

Consider the landscape. "You've got to remember how it was for musicians in the 1920s and 1930s," said William Ivey of the Country Music Foundation. "It was a whole different subculture than music is today. Musicians were almost outcasts. Even where they were accepted, you wouldn't have wanted your sister to marry one."

The traveling musician—black or white—during those days didn't have the liberty of concentrating on any particular musical form. If he wanted to eat regularly, he played what the people wanted to hear. For the bluesman, that meant playing an occasional hillbilly number or one of the popular songs of the day. Lillie Mae Glover, who sang and still sings the blues around Memphis, remembers that some of her most requested numbers were hillbilly songs, and that she sang them with all the panache of the blues. Bluesman Furry Lewis, one of the best-known veterans of the Delta blues, has a repertory that consists of the blues, story songs such as "Casey Jones," popular dance music of the 1920s, 1930s, and 1940s, a few hillbilly songs, and one or two old standards.

The white musician of the time felt the same pinch. Arthel "Doc" Watson picked up his first musical instrument in 1934, when he found a fretless banjo, hand-carved by his uncle. Blind since birth, Doc Watson became an omnivorous collector of musical repertory, beginning with the local music around his home in the mountains of Deep Gap, North Carolina. Not surprisingly, that music was black *and* white—blues and the string band music, hillbilly music. After becoming a local celebrity, Doc Watson donned an electric guitar and went on the road, during the important years of the 1940s.

He played everything from contemporary swing, such as the Western Swing of Bob Wills and big-band dance music, to rhythm and blues, to hillbilly music. He had to play what the people wanted to hear. "Every country musician I've ever listened to has influenced my style," he said, and for him, country included everything from mountain ballads to the blues. "Oh man, I am a dear lover of the blues. I've played a few shows with Furry

Lewis, and was on the same bill with Mississippi John
Hurt and Skip James. Somehow, I never could get the
soul in my guitar picking that they do, I didn't think. I
always found a place to criticize my music when I started
playing with them boys."

Since his "discovery" at the Newport Folk Festival in
the early 1960s Doc Watson has been hailed not only as a
brilliant and unique guitarist but as an important store-
house of information about the early days on the road
and the interchange betwen black and white musicians.

One of the reasons that interchange has not been documented, adds William Ivey, is that "people have come at
it either as a fan of the blues or as a fan of country.
They've refused to see the shared repertory between the
early hillbilly musicians and the early blues musicians,
and they've refused to acknowledge that there *was* social
interaction, even at the very height of segregation."

Much of that shared repertory from the 1940s was run
down by researcher Tony Russell in the late 1960s, and it
included such categories as story songs ("Casey Jones,"
"John Henry," "Stagger Lee," "Frankie and Johnny");
gambling and low-down living songs ("Don't Let the
Deal Go Down," "Ain't Nobody's Business," "Mama
Don't Allow"); the road and its loneliness, a special prov-
ince of the blues singers ("A Hundred Miles," "K.C.
Moan"); standards ("Turkey in the Straw," "Buffalo
Gals"); blues standards ("Walk Right In," "Corinna,
Corinna"); old hymns ("Give Me That Old Time Re-
ligion," "No Hiding Place Down There"); *really* old stan-
dards such as "It Ain't Gonna Rain No More"; and such
current instrumental blues compositions as "St. Louis
Blues" and "Beale Street Blues" by W. C. Handy. Even
Russell underestimates the contribution of the bluesmen.

White pickers would swipe a blues song just as fast as black pickers would memorize the latest hillbilly piece, and the song could be readily added to their sets with a minimum amount of work. And you might add to that list the spirituals, camp-meeting songs, and anything else the singer happened on in his travels. The operative word was versatility, and each audience was a new mountain to be climbed.

The traveling singer brought about several changes in the music and the society, all of them important to the rock and roll that was to come. First, they spread the influence around—a new black song sung by a white singer could make its way across the country in a few months, only to be picked up and brought home by a totally different route. The wandering singers also laid the groundwork for modern country music, which was vitally important to the development of popular music in the 1950s and 1960s. Finally, the singers managed to create what I call bar music, a melange of everything played with a beat you can dance to.

Southern bar music, the music of the honky-tonks and dives, was an entirely different animal from, say, swing or rhythm and blues, although the forms shared a number of elements. Bar music evolved from the hodgepodge of music that percolated through the South after the Civil War. Like the traveling singers, bar music took a little bit of this and a little bit of that, a little bit of black and a little bit of white, juggled it all together and came up with music just loud enough to keep you from thinking too much and to go right on ordering the whiskey.

The bars were called honky-tonks, a phrase that surfaced around the turn of the century in the Texas-Louisiana netherworld. Black bars in the New Orleans area were called "tonks," and the phrase was legitimized (by whites—what a surprise!) in a New York musical production called *Everything* in 1918, which featured (along with an appearance by Houdini) a number called "Everything Is Hunky Dory Down in Honky Tonk Town." Pretty soon the word *honky-tonk* was appearing everywhere, and everybody had the honky-tonk blues.

By the 1940s the honky-tonk had become a southern institution on a par with southern belles and mint juleps. Honky-tonks sprouted everywhere, from the edges of the booming cities to five miles removed from nowhere. Some sprouted meaner than others; some sprouted added attractions like cockfights or that newfangled invention, the jukebox, to augment the live music and the free-flowing liquor. When the soldiers came back from World War II, so changed from the country boys who left to fight, the honky-tonks entered their brief golden age. From the jukeboxes (the word "juke" is either from the African word for "black," meaning "evil," or from a notorious New York family of con men named Juke—take your pick) came an amalgam of hillbilly swing such as the music of Ernest Tubb, imitating his hero Jimmie Rodgers, Merle Kilgore, Roy Acuff, and the stars of the Grand Ole Opry in Nashville, and rhythm and blues hits by Fats Domino, John Lee Hooker, Lonnie Johnson, and other, more local acts. By the late 1940s independent record labels were producing products geared strictly to the jukebox trade in a specific area; an artist could be a huge star on his own turf, an unknown two hundred miles away.

The ambiguity in the music was firmly entrenched by the late 1940s. In fact, one of the great icons in country music, the legendary Jimmie Rodgers, was hardly more than a blues singer who happened to be white. Rodgers had been discovered at a recording session in Bristol, Tennessee, in 1927, staged by southern music pioneer Ralph Peer for the Victor Company. That same recording session in early August also produced the Carter Family, making it probably the single most important session in the history of country music. While Rodgers' repertoire was hardly limited to blues (remember, at that time *no* singer who hoped to make a living could be locked into any one form), he was a master of the blues form and of the yodel, for which he is best known. That yodel has just about driven music scholars batty, since nobody can figure out where it came from. Ace Memphis State University musicologist David Evans, who has devoted much of his life to minding the blues, calls the Rodgers yodel a cross between the Swiss-German yodel and the African falsetto at the end of a line. "There's two things going on with Jimmie Rodgers," he says. "There's the yodel used as a refrain, which is a standard vaudeville usage from the late teens and early 1920s, and there's the use of falsetto at the end of each sung line, which is more typical of black technique. And even then, Rodgers was not necessarily the first to adapt the Swiss-German yodel to the blues—vaudeville singers had already done that."

Legend has it that Jimmie Rodgers met Chester Burnett on the road one night, and upon hearing Burnett's distinctive "howl," called the black singer "Howlin' Wolf," a name that Chester Burnett carried for the rest of his life.

By the 1940s, though, the torch had passed to a new honky-tonk hero named Hank Williams. Like the greatest bluesmen, Hank Williams had a life that belongs more to the province of mythology than reality. A whole generation of southerners remember the exact day, the very moment when they first saw Hank Williams sing. They remember his hang-dog expression and his high, lonesome sound. They remember his way with the ladies and his seven encores for "Lovesick Blues" at the Grand Ole Opry. His life has been dissected, analyzed a dozen different ways, and run through a few doctoral dissertations, and the only sure facts are that he drank, took drugs, wrote some of the most brilliant music ever written in this country, and died on New Year's Day 1953.

I recently collaborated on the autobiography of his only son, Hank Williams, Jr.—an excellent songwriter in his own right—and one thing that came through after many weeks on the road with him was that Hank Williams, Sr., was *still* an important part of people's lives. It's not unusual to walk into some five-and-dime honky-tonk in the middle of nowhere and find ole Hank still on the jukebox, right alongside Linda Ronstadt, John Denver, Moe Bandy, and hundreds of other performers singing Hank's songs.

Like James Dean, the rebel without a cause, Hank Williams seemed doomed from the start. He was not only a rebel without a cause, he was a rebel who could not rebel. His despair was a living, breathing creature, a constant reminder that despite stardom, despite money, his situation was as hopeless as that of the plain-dirt Alabama farmer who watched first the rain, then the lack of it, reduce his hopes and dreams to a handful of baked red dirt. All that was left was the all-too-brief solace of the honky-tonks.

The rise of Hank Williams and his band, the Drifting Cowboys, was the high-water mark of the honky-tonks.

By the time he played the Grand Ole Opry in 1948, Williams was a local star of such proportions that he totally dominated country music long past his death in 1953. His music of lost loves and lost souls legitimized the 'tonks and make them the place to be. They became, God forbid, fashionable in a way they had never been before. There are no recordings of Hank Williams' playing in the honky-tonks, although his band members and fans remember a much funkier music than the music of Hank Williams on record.

"His music was a lot closer to the blues, a lot closer to a swing beat, than the music he recorded later," said Chet Flippo, Hank Williams' most recent biographer. "The music was definitely a lot funkier—he even took horns on the road with him. It was all dance music."

It's easy to say (and it has been said numerous times) that the blues tradition in country music died with Jimmie Rodgers, although nothing could be further from the truth. Rather than try to follow the blues through the white men who sang them, it's more important to follow the beat. While Hank Williams might not have been singing classic blues, he was keeping the black beat alive, though not because he had an overwhelming love of blacks. Although he had learned music from a black street singer named Rufe Payne—Tee-Tot, as he was known in Montgomery, Alabama—Williams kept the beat because it made people feel good, made their bodies sway, their blood run hot, and the deadening reality of another day in the fields seem far away. He knew the blues as a living creature, something that came 'round at midnight, and he didn't need to ask whether it was all right for a white man to be singing them.

The black thread in country music was never really lost, only forgotten, as it would be forgotten in the rock and roll fury that was just around the corner after Hank Williams. In fact, the ubiquitous southern bar music was the *direct* ancestor of rock and roll, the ultimate fusion of black and white. Rhythm and blues was *too* black, too alien to the experience of white southerners. Hillbilly music was becoming too fixed in the Grand Ole Opry mold, too inflexible, almost genteel—the Opry even shunned Williams because he drank and "set a bad example." He would not have been allowed to play the kind of music he played in the honky-tonks on the stage of the Grand Ole Opry. But the music of the honky-tonks *was* the music of the South, and virtually everybody was familiar with it. It lay like a pine forest at the height of the summer, waiting for a spark to set off the roaring inferno that could happen in minutes. That music is still there, still absorbing influences the way the Chinese absorbed invaders. In later chapters we'll see how that music exploded in Memphis to become rock and roll and, years later, give birth to southern rock *à la* the Allman Brothers Band.

Country music retains its importance today because it is slow to change and prone to reflect accurately the lives of its fans. Country music can change, as it has changed in the last five years, and still remain the same at its heart. Willie Nelson can, after twenty years in the business, suddenly expand his audience to include refugees from the Woodstock Nation without changing his music one iota. Waylon Jennings can become the biggest star in country music since Hank Williams by remaining true to the beat. In fact, folks call Waylon's distinct guitar-playing style "chicken pickin'." Before Waylon, the plunky style was known as "nigger pickin'," because that's the way many of the old bluesmen played.

Country is the music that is acted upon, the flip side of black music. Whether it's Ray Charles shocking the music world of the 1950s by going to Nashville to record country music ("Busted," "I Can't Stop Loving You") or Ronnie Milsap, one of the biggest names in country music today, playing piano behind Smokey Robinson and the Miracles and Bobby "Blue" Bland in Atlanta, country and black music have remained inextricably linked, something the musicians have never forgotten.

A FEW HOURS
BEFORE SUNRISE

Rock and roll provided us with a release and a justification that we had never dreamt of.

> —Peter Guralnick,
> *Feel Like Going Home*

Again, the white man took from the black, but this time he gave something in return.

> —Jerry Hopkins,
> *The Rock Story*

With the advent of the rock and roll historian, the trend has been to denigrate the rise of Sun Records in Memphis and to emphasize instead the numerous other "rock moments." To be sure, in the early 1950s rock and roll was beginning to boil all over the country. The rise of such almost-rock acts as Fats Domino, whose New Orleans music constantly approached the rock boundary (if

90

such a thing can be said to exist) and then fell back, and Clyde McPhatter and vocal harmony groups, generally lumped together as doo-wop, signaled a major change in popular tastes among young people. Something, as Bob Dylan would later observe, was happening. Nobody, though, was yet sure what.

The reason for the critical slighting of Sun has as much to do with historical nit-picking as with the sad decline of Elvis Presley in later years. And there was no small touch of regional bias at work—rockabilly was a distinctly southern phenomenon, springing from the fertile soul of the South, where black and white had, however painfully, intermixed for years. There has been a strong retrospective push for regional equality, lest Memphis cop all the credit. New Orleans was and is a world unto itself, molded by international influences that never touched the rest of the South, and its music has always been a few degrees off center. Doo-wop grew up in Los Angeles and the urbanized Northeast; Chicago had its electric blues and, later, the authentic genius of Chuck Berry.

But while it's quite easy to identify a rock moment here and a rock moment there, it's important not to lose sight of the fact that it was rockabilly—the music of Sam Phillips and Elvis Presley—that set the tone for rock. Rockabilly, with its balanced exuberance and fury, its tension between blues and country, black and white, plucked a chord that is still vibrating strongly. It was rockabilly that decreed rock and roll should be more than just fun; that rock was a revolution in lifestyle as well. On that count, the other branches of the rock family failed.

The decade of the 1950s was primed like a time bomb with only minutes left until detonation. The late 1940s were dominated by the crooners, such as Frank Sinatra, Tony Bennett, and Perry Como, and country singers, including Hank Williams, Hank Snow, and Tennessee Ernie Ford. Novelty songs headed the charts—1950 alone numbered among its gold records "Frosty the Snow Man" by Gene Autry, "Rag Mop" by the Ames Brothers, "If I Knew You Were Coming I'd Have Baked a Cake" by Eileen Barton, "The Thing" by Phil Harris, "Peter Cottontail" by Merv Shriner, and "Hot Canary" by violinist Florian Zabach.

But by 1950 something else was making itself felt on the "race" charts. Black music, long tied to the blues, had mutated, and the offspring, rhythm and blues, appeared to be viable. Rhythm and blues, being essentially danceable blues, had long been a staple of the southern honkytonks. Borrowing the beat from gospel music and the subject matter (sex) from the blues, the rhythm and blues player generated excitement, and the new music spread with the diaspora of blacks from the South to the mechanized North. While many found a better life than they had left behind, many others exchanged one niggertown for another. The blues had been at home in the rural South, but rhythm and blues flourished in the bright lights of the city. The blues did become citified as more and more of the old blues players found their way north. Chicago especially began to bloom, attracting the very cream of Memphis with the lure of a new life. The archetypal story, of course, concerns Muddy Waters, who left for Chicago in 1943.

Born McKinley Morganfield in Rolling Fork, Mississippi, on April 4, 1915, Muddy Waters was playing the blues by the time he was fifteen years old. He worked in the Delta around Memphis for years, performing unamplified blues. Much of his early work was unabashedly derivative, borrowing from such blues greats as Robert Johnson and the hundreds of other singers who made their home in the Mississippi Delta. In fact, he was recorded for the Library of Congress in the early 1940s by folk music researcher Alan Lomax.

In 1943 Muddy Waters joined the increasing number of blacks who fled the rural poverty of the South to take a job at a paper mill in Chicago while trying to make it as a blues singer at night. But the music that seemed right for the cotton fields of Mississippi didn't fit the mechanized world of the factories. For one thing, it was too *quiet*. For people who spent their days in the grinding machine noise of the urban world, shouted blues and an acoustic guitar just didn't make it. They wanted to talk and dance and get rowdy, have a few drinks and forget the war and the work and as much of the world as possible. Like the traveling singers of years before, the new urban bluesman was given the Darwinian ultimatum—adapt or perish.

In 1944 Muddy Waters purchased his first electric guitar and, in 1947, was introduced to the Chess Brothers, Leonard and Phil, two white Jewish men who ran a rhythm and blues record label in Chicago. Muddy Waters became the high priest of electrified blues, and the Chess Brothers were his most ardent supporters. Waters popularized the idea of the electric blues band, playing loud and hard and with all the energy it was possible to summon up, while sticking as close as possible to the old blues formulas.

This was the very tradition that the "new" music, rock and roll, would soon tap to its benefit, borrowing from such Muddy Waters classics as "Hoochie Coochie Man,"

"Mannish Boy," "Got My Mojo Working," and "I Feel Like Going Home." In 1954 Waters wrote and recorded a song called "Rollin' Stone," which would later inspire Bob Dylan to write "Like a Rolling Stone," an English "blues" group to name themselves after the song, and a magazine to follow suit.

By the 1950s Muddy Waters was a legend not just in Chicago but across the country as well. The Chess Brothers, along with the Bihari Brothers in Los Angeles, Sam Phillips in Memphis, and numerous other independent labels that sprang up in the late 1940s, had succeeded in *nationalizing* rhythm and blues. The traveling singer had been superseded by the jukebox, and the independent labels were cranking out jukebox fodder like there was no tomorrow. The result was the rise of national rhythm and blues stars—Muddy Waters, Ivory Joe Hunter, Fats Domino (as mentioned earlier), John Lee Hooker (who had two million-sellers, "I'm in the Mood" and "Boogie Chillun," in 1948 alone), Joe Turner, and other lesser lights.

But the national spotlight didn't shine on the new bluesmen too long, because the stage was finally set for the rise of the new music. Ironically, it would be Muddy Waters himself who would help drive the nails into his music's coffin by introducing the Chess Brothers to a different sort of rhythm and blues man named Chuck Berry. But before Chuck Berry, and before Sam Phillips and Elvis Presley, there was the craze for vocal group harmonies—doo-wop—the first sign that the world was getting ready to go bonkers.

When we think of doo-wop, we probably think about the vocal group music from 1954 to 1959, when the most famous doo-wop material hit the charts. The reason it's called doo-wop—and what distinguishes it from plain old group harmony—is that not everybody in the group sang the same words. The harmony part consisted of nonsense syllables ("doo-wop" being the favorite).

As was the case with Muddy Waters' electrified blues, technology had a hand in the rise of doo-wop. Numerous independent record companies had acted to create a sort of self-fulfilling prophecy—by trying to meet the needs of what they perceived as a national market, they were helping to create that very market. It was a classic case of the supply-demand-supply cycle of economics. Consequently, the *bottom line* entered the picture: the more cheaply a record was made, the less chance the company had of getting stung. Cheap records meant big profits, and the cheapest records to make were vocal harmony records.

Vocal harmony groups could dispense with much of the expensive instrumentation required by solo singers. Perhaps more importantly, the groups were so hungry that record company owners could dispense with the onerous task of paying them large (or indeed, any) sums. The results were cheap records, high profits, and hundreds upon hundreds of vocal harmony records flooding the market.

While doo-wop is considered by many experts to be a subgenre of rhythm and blues, that is perhaps oversimplifying the matter. It is true that doo-wop sprang from that long-lasting black tradition of harmony groups, and as we saw in an earlier chapter, harmony groups played a huge role in the formation of modern gospel music. Indeed, since slavery days blacks had used their voices as substitutes for nonexistent (or proscribed) musical instruments (the banned African drum, for example).

The immediate antecedents of doo-wop were two enormously successful black groups of the late 1940s, the Mills Brothers and the Ink Spots. The Mills, four brothers from Piqua, Ohio, began recording in the big-band era of the early 1940s and scored such big-band–oriented hits as "Paper Doll" and "You Always Hurt the One You Love." The Ink Spots, the more durable and older of the two groups, turned out hits regularly in the late 1930s and throughout the 1940s, including work they did with Ella Fitzgerald. They were originally porters at New York City's Paramount Theater when they were "discovered" in 1937. Their first hit ("If I Didn't Care") came two years later. Prophetically, the Ink Spots became famous for their spoken choruses, a device that would later evolve into the doo-wop harmonies.

Finally, doo-wop was a way of avoiding the bluesman's burden for young black kids seeking to make it in the music business. The blues, even electric blues à la Muddy Waters and its more danceable cousins, required a fierce element of commitment. By tradition and thanks to the cold, hard realities of life on the road, the blues and rhythm and blues were more a way of life than a profession. The dictum of the blues—life is short, pain much, pleasures few—was hardly conducive to a good-time Saturday night. Then, too, the blues were already becoming old-fashioned, a reminder of a time and way of life many urban blacks would just as soon forget. As the new generation of urban-reared blacks came of age, hard times in the South seemed further and further away. There was a new wind blowing, and it was blowing the blues away.

Most importantly, perhaps—at least to the groups

themselves—was that if you sang vocal harmonies instead of the blues, you might become a *star* via the wonderful media of radio and records. Not just a star in the "race" market, but a star on the pop charts, like the Mills Brothers or the Ink Spots. To some extent—though much more has been made of this than the facts warrant—doo-wop offered black groups their first taste of national stardom. By 1951 black harmony groups, led by the Orioles and the Ravens, were dominating the black rhythm and blues charts. The first doo-wop record to cross over from the black rhythm and blues charts to the white pop charts was "Sixty Minute Man" in late 1951, recorded by the Dominoes, featuring vocalist Clyde McPhatter. It wasn't until 1953, though, that the proverbial walls came tumbling down, and that was when a Cleveland disc jockey named Alan Freed began playing doo-wop songs on his radio show for white kids. Freed was an authentic original, the first of the wild-men rock and roll disc jockeys. On his late-night *Moondog Show* on WJW in Cleveland Freed, himself a fan of rhythm and blues, began programming the previously all-black music for his overwhelmingly white audience. Hedging his bets, he decided to call the music "rock and roll" rather than "rhythm and blues," picking up the phrase from the floating body of blues lyrics that had apparently been around since Day One. As early as 1952 Freed knew he was on to something big, maybe the biggest thing ever, and with the increasing waves of doo-wop to choose from, the Freed phenomenon—programming black music for white kids—began spreading.

Doo-wop, originally the child of the urban Northeast and the West Coast, began spreading, and by 1954 it dominated the pop charts. That year brought "Gee" by the Crows (yet another song in the sweepstakes of Name the First Rock and Roll Record) and "Earth Angel," perhaps the quintessential doo-wop record, by the Penguins. (In the 1950s naming these groups after birds seemed *cute,* but then, so did poodle skirts.) Also in 1954 came the first important "cover" (a white group's recording of a black song)—the Crew Cuts' recording of "Sh-Boom," originally cut by the Chords. It triggered a wave of cover versions.

Rock critics have made as much of covers as of doo-wop, the most prevalent theory being that the cover versions were just another example of white ripping off black. Well, maybe, but here is where the whole doo-wop-as-the-beginning-of-rock theory begins to spring leaks. The wave of white covers was as much a function of big stealing from little as white from black. Many of the songs covered had been put out by small record companies, which didn't have the resources to fight back legally when their material was ripped off. Also, vocal harmony was hardly an exclusively black tradition. Once doo-wop was established on the charts and white groups began adding their own material, it was literally impossible to tell what color a group was simply by listening to them. In the South, where I grew up, the very key to doo-wop's success was its racial anonymity. Since it was not clearly identifiable as "nigger" music, it was acceptable in a time of legal segregation. Even the more rhythm-and-blues–oriented groups, such as the Robins and later the Coasters (fueled by two white songwriters, Jerry Leiber and Mike Stoller, about whom more later), hardly carried the black imprint of, say, Muddy Waters or even Joe Turner (who recorded the original "Shake, Rattle and Roll," copied with such success by Bill Haley and his

Saddlemen, soon to be the Comets). The year 1954 marked the turning point in more ways than one, because it can safely be called the year a boy rocked and the world rolled. Rhythm and blues was riding high with Hank Ballard and the Midnighters, Fats Domino, and Guitar Slim. Doo-wop was an established force. In April of that year Bill Haley, the former country and western singer who had changed his tune after watching some kids dance to rhythm and blues records, recorded two rock classics—Joe Turner's "Shake, Rattle and Roll" and "Rock Around the Clock," which was featured the next year in the movie *The Blackboard Jungle*. In July of 1954 Elvis Presley would walk into Sam Phillips' small studio in Memphis, Tennessee, to record "That's All Right, Mama," and it was too late to turn back.

The big winner in the deemphasis of Sun Records in recent years has been rock and roll's *other* endearing and enduring legend, Chuck Berry. Berry was born in St. Louis, Missouri, in 1931, and lived a fairly normal childhood broken by a three-year stint in reform school for attempted robbery. By the time he left reform school, he was the model of propriety, having nailed down a degree in hairdressing and cosmetology, and he settled down with a new family to work on an assembly line. But he had also learned the guitar along the way, and the music business pulled him like a magnet. During a trip to Chicago in 1955 he sat in on a session with Muddy Waters, who was extremely impressed by the young black guitarist's skill and imagination. At Waters' urging, Berry met with Phil and Leonard Chess, who were sufficiently impressed to get him into a studio. The first two cuts he made were the bluesy "Wee Wee Hours" and a country-styled song Berry had worked out titled "Ida Mae." The

Chess Brothers were less than thrilled with that title so Berry renamed his song "Maybellene," and his career was off and running. Interestingly enough, Alan Freed's name appears on "Maybellene" as a co-author. In these cynical times it's easy to write off his authorship as pure payola, and in truth Freed played the hell out of the record and was largely responsible for breaking "Maybellene" nationally. Yet at least one author, Charlie Gillett in *The Sound of the City,* suggests that Freed's contributions were more solid and that "Maybellene," through his ministrations, owes a debt to Bill Haley and the Comets. If we tinker with it long enough, this stuff can get hideously complicated.

Nevertheless, Berry produced some of rock's classic songs—"Sweet Little Sixteen," "Roll Over Beethoven," "School Day," "Johnny B. Goode," "Rock & Roll Music," "Promised Land," "Nadine," "Almost Grown," "Memphis, Tennessee," and many others. His secret was that, like the doo-wop kings, he had found a way to transcend race. His touchstone was the blending of white country and black blues. Berry's guitar work was straight country filtered through rhythm and blues (listen to any rock record and you'll still hear the basic formula), and his vocals were the exact opposite of the slurred, idiosyncratic performances common to most other black music.

Either consciously or subconsciously Berry knew he couldn't push it *too* far; America would not yet stand for a real black man singing straight from the heart. Sophisticated minstrelsy, such as the super-smooth vocals of Nat "King" Cole, or novelty, as done by Fats Domino, were the trick. Without a trick, it was back to the anonymous colorlessness of the doo-wops. In short, to be black required a gimmick to stay alive, and Chuck Berry adopted the most novel (and most successful) gimmick of them all; he became the Eternal Teenager. With his sly winks, his duck walk, and his high-schools-girls-and-cars lyrics, Berry neatly sidestepped the question of race to tap the budding youth culture, fruit of the Baby Boom.

Even a gimmick wasn't enough ultimately. The final element necessary to turn rock into something other than just another musical fad was the element of rebellion, and that had to come from the whites themselves. Chuck Berry could slyly hint at it, and Little Richard Penniman, another black singer, could even shout it out, but the message wouldn't become real until it came from one of *us*, as opposed to one of *them*. Kids could dance to black music—or music performed by blacks—even go crazy over the music and the singer, but they'd danced and gone crazy before over the likes of Frank Sinatra.

A fusion had to take place; a white boy had to sing the blues. There had to be an Elvis.

HISTORICAL INTERLUDE

This is what happened on Beale Street one winter evening in 1954.

The weather was cold, a wet, icy cold that seeped right through the heaviest of coats and cut straight to the bone. The young man loitering on Hernando Street wasn't wearing a coat, and was obviously freezing. He paced back and forth in front of a small doorway, swinging his gangly arms back and forth, trying to ward off the cold. He was wearing a bright pink suit that clashed terribly with his pale blue complexion. The pink suit seemed two sizes too big, giving him the look of a scarecrow. His belt and shoes were white patent leather, and the shoes showed all the signs of having spent many an evening walking the hard, unforgiving pavement of Beale Street.

The few other people on the street that particular evening stared openly at the pink suit, even more intently when they realized that the young man in it was white, some kind of jive asshole standing near the corner of Beale and Hernando, freezing his tail off, not even wearing an overcoat.

His pacing was obsessive, faster and faster, in time with the wad of gum he was chewing. His hair was slicked back, and a lock of the greased pompadour kept falling across his eyes. He pushed it back in place without seeming to notice.

Finally, the small door opened and a caramel-colored face peered out into the cold.

"Elvis," the black man said into the gathering dark. "Elvis, goddamnit boy! Are you ready or not? C'mon, boy!"

Elvis Presley quickly spat the gum into the gutter of Hernando Street and hurried over to the black man at the door. He pushed the slicked hair back into place for the umpteenth time, and his angular face broke into a wide grin.

"I'm sorry," said Elvis Presley. "I guess you caught me just dreamin' some, trying to keep warm." He was earnest, apologetic.

"You don't watch out, boy, you get both our butts in the Memphis City Jail," the proprietor said. It was against the law for a white man to enter a black entertainment establishment (and even more against the law for a black man to enter a white entertainment establishment). Separate but equal was the byword, the way to keep the black men away from the white women, God forbid, and vice versa.

The proprietor looked up and down the street, which was practically deserted in the evening chill.

"C'mon," he said, pushing Elvis ahead of him up the narrow back staircase, "c'mon in."

The two went up the back stairs, into the Club Handy through the emergency exit. Although the night was still relatively young, the joint was already cooking, the steamy heat of moving bodies absorbing the winter cold. The feature attraction that night was just the house band, a group that usually fronted for local rhythm and blues singer Bill Harvey, and they'd worked the crowd into a white heat.

Elvis entered the club, and a ripple of indignation moved through the crowd. There were special expressions, special masks, reserved for white people, and the majority of the faces slipped automatically into those expressions—smooth brown masks, neither frowning nor smiling, eyes that soon turned away. A few of the faces registered resentment, disgust. Another white boy, the faces said, come here to our ground to look and steal what he can, maybe leave tonight with a sleek brown woman on his elbow; ought to keep his white ass off Beale Street. The other faces showed amusement; eyes met and exchanged secret signals, totally lost on the young man in the pink suit. Look at him, the eyes winked back and forth, poor little white boy who wants to be a nigger.

Elvis blinked in the smoky room, licked his lips and cleared his throat. His body, betraying his uneasiness, began moving to the music. The proprietor left his side and walked over to the bandstand, where he corraled the bandleader between numbers. There was much whispering between the two, with a few gestures and strange glances back at Elvis, who waited quietly by the rear door. Finally the bandleader laughed and motioned for Elvis to come over to the bandstand.

"Folks," the bandleader said to the attentive audience, "we got us a special treat tonight. Mr. Elvis Presley here, who works for Mr. Sam Phillips over at Sun Records, is gonna sing us a couple of songs. C'mon up here, boy!"

Elvis smiled and waved, and the crowd responded with thunderous (not necessarily good-natured) applause and laughter.

"Thank you very much," Elvis said, turning to the band. "Let's sing some blues here. You boys know Sleepy John Estes' 'Milkcow Blues Boogie'?"

The bandleader snorted, and before Elvis turned around, the band dug into a hopped-up version of the blues standard.

The band was puzzled. Elvis wasn't singing what they were playing, at least not the right way. The beat was not the same—he was singing ahead of the jazzed-up blues beat, moving his body to punctuate the rhythm in his head. The band shifted tempo a bit, but something was still wrong, strangely, undefinably *wrong*.

The crowd sensed that the band and the singer were not together, but they were already moving to the white boy's new rhythm. It was somehow more fierce and less worldly than the dance music they were used to, more akin to the frantic honky-tonk blues than the classy Club Handy. Elvis finished up to a scattering of applause. He was flushed, cocky, looking down from the stage into a sea of eyes and teeth. He pushed his hair back from his sweating face and sneered at the audience.

"Thank you thank you," he said. "Let's do some Big Boy Crudup now. Boys," he said to the band, "follow me now."

The band fumbled around, blind men looking for the new beat . . .

It was almost as if he *couldn't* sing rhythm and blues. His body jerked as the song poured out, leaner and meaner than anything Big Boy Crudup ever imagined . . .

The crowd moved with the new beat, hypnotized by the swaying figure in the pink suit, looking deep into a pink crystal ball showing a pink vision of the future, a pink and white vision of the future . . .

The band stumbled again, reaching for the beat. The band members were consummate professionals, veterans of a million hours in a million smoky clubs, but this music was something different, so close to what they were used to playing that it made playing it difficult. The fingers want the old familiar patterns . . .

The applause after the song was uneasy, but Elvis couldn't feel it. The music in his head went round and round, and he knew in his heart and in his soul and in his guts that it was the music of the future, if anybody would just listen to it. He would find a way to make Mr. Sam Phillips understand if it took the rest of his life, because he knew he had the power. He knew that he, a white truck driver from Tupelo, Mississippi, had the beat. Just like the crowd at the Club Handy knew, down in their guts, that they'd just seen someone step on their graves.

THE UBANGI STOMP

Hell, that's different. That's a pop song now, Little Vi. That's good.

—Sam Phillips to Elvis Presley,
Monday, July 5, 1954

Nothing in traditional American music is as white as it may seem, or as black. . . . The searcher of ethnic purity . . . finds little.
—Nick Tosches, writing in
The Illustrated History of Country Music

No doubt about it, history's got a hold of Sam Phillips, and it's shaking him the way an old dog might shake a greasy rag. On my desk as I write are seven books, three magazines, and one videotape, each lovingly recounting that fateful meeting at Sun Records, 706 Union Avenue, Memphis, Tennessee, on the afternoon of July 5, 1954 (or July 4 or July 6, take your choice), when Sam Phillips

106

and Elvis Presley conspired knowingly and willfully to create rock and roll and topple the world. Off the top of my head I can think of a dozen more books and God knows how many magazine articles, newspaper series, and doctoral dissertations faithfully devoted to that afternoon when the white boy rocked and the world rolled.

The reasons for this incredible outpouring of words and pictures are many and varied, but they are all bound up in this single fact: Each of us, on one level or the other, was changed by what happened in Memphis that July afternoon. The world since then has been slightly askew, its spiritual orbit shifted. Because of that event, wrote Greil Marcus in *Rolling Stone,* "the future has possibilities that otherwise would have been foreclosed." It is seldom that history and fate conspire to give us a single point that we can look back on and say, "There. It changed *then.*" We clutch the event to our hearts and try to wring the truth from it, as if by staring again and again at it we might discover, once and for all, what we have become.

The aftershock of Elvis' death on August 16, 1977, surpassed everyone's wildest imagination. The *haute-culture* critics in the cities were stunned: What had this fat, sick, middle-aged man done to warrant this national expression of grief? Not since John Kennedy lay cradled in his wife's arms in a limousine in Dallas, not since Martin King laid down his cross within sight of Beale Street, had the country been drawn together into such mourning.

We have serious trouble approaching that July afternoon in Memphis because we are still too close to it, the ramifications are still too fresh in our minds. We can choose to approach Elvis coolly, like culture maven Tom Wolfe, who in a recent issue of *Esquire* magazine called

Elvis "a Valentino for poor whites. . . . A genuine Tupelo boy raised on drop-biscuits, loose sausage, Nabs & Coke, had entered Show Business heaven." Or we can approach the revolution at 706 Union Avenue with pencil and notebook in hand, prepared to tell over and over again—for the record—what *really* happened there. We can ferret out the positions of all the switches on Sam Phillips' sound board; we can ascertain for posterity how many Cokes Elvis had to drink before he ripped into "Blue Moon of Kentucky" and "That's All Right, Mama," and Sam Phillips came running out of the tiny control room, his excitement bubbling to the bursting point, calling out to Elvis, "Hell, that's different! That's a pop song now, Little Vi. That's *good!*"

The problem, though, with turning what happened in Memphis into a college course—say, American Music 101, meets twice a week—is that it's impossible to translate a generalized *feeling* into a concise, fact-by-fact recitation. Sometimes a factual history only serves to obscure what really happened. Here are two examples.

When William D. Miller, a noted and quite thorough historian, wrote the "definitive" history of Boss Crump, *Mr. Crump of Memphis,* Crump came out just this side of the angels. The Crump machine was miraculously free of dirty money, niggers, and whores, and Miller concentrated on Boss Crump's undeniable contributions to the city of Memphis (for example, he founded the Memphis Audubon Society of Birdwatchers on the day he ordered the whorehouses closed).

Or take the very history of Beale Street itself. Every politician in Memphis from about 1950 forward can proudly point to what he did to "save" Beale Street and solve the "problem"—everyone's posterior is well covered. Only that's not what happened at all. The "facts" point in one direction, the reality is somewhere else entirely. And so it is with July 5, 1954, in Memphis. The more we sift through the minutiae of the climactic birth of rock and roll, the less we really seem to know. It is, writes Peter Guralnick in *Lost Highway,* a classic example of the Heisenberg Uncertainty Principle in action: In observing an object, the very act of observation affects the object being observed.

One final barrier stands between us and a true understanding of what happened in Memphis that July: the world has changed since then.

In one of the more depressing events of my journalistic life I rode with Charlie Rich from Chicago to Memphis on his private plane, en route to a special concert to open a new state park near his hometown of Colt, Arkansas. Rich was riding the height of his country music and pop success with such ballads (sometimes unkindly referred to as "elevator music") as "Behind Closed Doors" and "Most Beautiful Girl," but the Charlie Rich I wanted to talk to was the one whose voice I remembered coming out of the jukebox at my grandfather's drugstore in Memphis, the one who sang "Lonely Weekends" and "Mohair Sam" so soulfully you'd almost have sworn he was black.

So I cornered Charlie in the back of his plane, where he was soaking up a glass of milk to mitigate the higher-proof stuff in his stomach, and began dive-bombing him with questions. Why did he change? Why did he stop singing the blues? Why had he become a country crooner? Actually, I asked one question in a whole bunch of different forms: Why, I demanded to know, aren't you the same as you were in 1959?

He looked tired, and hurt, and for a long time he didn't say anything at all. Finally he answered.

"I don't know," Charlie Rich said. "I guess you just start doing something and . . . I just don't know. Time passes."

When we finally got to Colt, it was hot enough for what grass there was to just pop up out of the ground to keep from frying. Everybody within a ten-mile radius had come to see their favorite son perform. The stage was a flatbed truck with a piano on it, and after a quick medley of hits Charlie paused and looked out at the audience. "Maybe," he said, "some of you remember these." For the next two hours, in the blasted heat of that Arkansas afternoon, Charlie Rich played the blues, until his clothes were soaked through with sweat and the people backstage were talking about "going out there and carrying that damn fool off before he has a heart attack!" His voice rolled out of that Mickey Mouse PA system like honey and I sat in that cow pasture transfixed, with tears in my eyes.

When he finished and walked offstage, the woman next to me turned to her husband and said, "I wish he'd done more of his hits and less of that nigger stuff."

Just as the blues weren't born on Beale Street, rock and roll wasn't really born at 706 Union Avenue. Identifying the first "real" rock and roll record is lots of fun as a party game, but it's about as useful as counting the number of angels that can dance on the head of a pin. Music in the early 1950s was boiling all over the country, and like birds in the path of a hurricane, *everybody* knew *some-*

thing was getting ready to happen. Obsessive British researcher Charlie Gillett, in his landmark book, *The Sound
of the City,* isolated no fewer than *five* different kinds of
rock stewing in those early Eisenhower years: northern
band rock and roll, as in Bill Haley with his spitcurl and
"Rock Around the Clock"; Pat Boone and his remark-
ably successful covers of R & B hits such as "Ain't That a
Shame" and "Tutti Frutti"; Chicago rhythm and blues,
mainly Chuck Berry and Bo Diddley; vocal group rock,
such as the Orioles ("Crying in the Chapel"), the Charms
("Hearts of Stone"), and the Penguins ("Earth Angel");
and finally, whatever it was that was happening in
Memphis.

This is where it gets all mixed up with color. Obviously, Bill Haley, Elvis Presley, and Pat Boone were
white, and the music from Chicago was black, as were
most of the vocal groups. The *real* breakdown, though,
goes something like this: The only real black singers of
the bunch were Berry and Bo Diddley, who were clear
flukes. Even so, they always played second fiddle to the
white rockers who followed them. The secret of the black
vocal groups was to sound neither white nor black—listen
to any oldies show if you don't believe that. The vocal
groups were ringers, a carrying forward of an old vocal
tradition that knew no color. Pat Boone and Bill Haley
were clearly *imitating* black acts, Boone because it made
him piles and piles of money (and his success didn't hurt
Fats Domino and Little Richard, either), Haley because
he saw that his audiences were hungry for music they
could dance to, like the black jump blues records that
were getting wider and wider distribution. But beneath
the surface, both Boone and Haley were representatives
of an older tradition, that of the crooners. Both were

consummate entertainers, dedicated to giving the audience what it wanted, whether that was "Love Letters in
the Sand" or "Shake, Rattle, and Roll" (cleaned up, of
course, since the Devil in nylon hose was hardly acceptable subject matter for white kids, at least not back then).

At times, Haley seemed almost bemused by the fury
that was building around him. He *sang* rock and roll; he
didn't *believe* it.

Which leaves Elvis and whatever it was that was happening at Sam Phillips' studio at 706 Union, and perhaps a little of that oft-repeated history is in order here.

Sam Phillips arrived in Memphis in 1945, a young disc
jockey from Florence, Alabama. He had grown up in the
cotton fields, and the blues were as much a part of his life
as if he'd been born black. But he hadn't been, and even
as a child he was aware of the difference. "So I think I
felt from the beginning the total inequity of man's inhu-
manity to his brother," Sam told Peter Guralnick. "It
took on the aspect with me that someday I would act on
my feelings, I would show them on an individual, one-to-
one basis."

In 1950 Sam got that chance. While working as a disc
jockey at WREC, he was also working as a promoter for
bands at the swank Hotel Peabody, a job that involved
some recording. He soon became enamored of recording,
of making *records,* and in 1950 he opened his own studio
over a radiator shop at 706 Union, determined to record
the multitude of black talent he heard every day on
Beale Street. He called his studio the Memphis Recording Service.

Beale Street was still brimming with talent, and pretty
soon Sam was working with a couple of popular disc
jockeys from the all-black (although white-owned)

WDIA—Rufus Thomas and Riley "Blues Boy" King, better known locally as B. B. King. The tapes he made were leased to more established independent labels, such as Chess in Chicago and Modern in Los Angeles, and in June 1951 Chess had a first hit with one of Sam's tapes, "Rocket 88" by Jackie Brenston, backed up by young Ike Turner's band. (In that cocktail party game of naming the first "real" rock record, "Rocket 88" will come up again and again. Later in 1951 the head of a country and western band called the Saddlemen, a guy named ·Bill Haley, heard "Rocket 88" and was so impressed that he cut a version of his own, his first noncountry recording.)

But Sam Phillips was too much the individualist to be happy working for someone else—especially given the cutthroat nature of the music business in those years. The cut he felt most keenly was the loss of Chester Burnett—the Howlin' Wolf—to Chess Records. The only solution was to take complete control himself, to establish a record label of his own. "I thought about it long and hard," Sam told interviewer Robert Palmer. "My devotion was in creating, or attempting to. I have a kind of evangelical way about me. I don't go for all this religion as it's structured today; my evangelism is, in my own peculiar way, letting people out of themselves. I got pure gratification, far more than what recompense I got monetarily, in unlocking or helping these people unlock their lives. So with the help of my old friend Jim Bullet, who had the Bullet label out of Nashville years ago, we started Sun."

The distinctive yellow label with its crowing rooster was designed by a friend from Florence, Alabama, and Sam was on his way. His first cut, a duet with Walter Horton and Jack Kelly, got such a poor reaction that it was never officially released, but later product fared much better. His first big hit came from deejay Rufus Thomas, an answer to Willie Mae Thornton's hit "Hound Dog" called "Bear Cat." A follow-up called "Tiger Man," complete with jungle noises and assorted howls, pretty much cemented Sun's place as a major rhythm and blues label. Sam recorded a prison group, the Prisonaires, Little Junior Parker and his Blue Flames, Memphis Ma Rainey, James Cotton, Doctor Ross (who had the "Boogie Disease"), Willie Nix, and some lesser known (actually totally unknown outside Sam Phillips' door) artists such as Hot Shot Love, whose weird cuts such as "Wolf Call Boogie" and "Harmonica Jam" today sound strangely up to date.

Sam had flirted with white blues—a white man singing in the distinctly black idioms, notably a white hobo named Harmonica Frank—but it wasn't until Elvis Presley stopped by the Memphis Recording Service (which Sam still maintained) to cut a record for his mother, Gladys, that history first started sniffing around Sam Phillips. Maybe Memphis was the only place in the world where what happened could have happened.

1. Beale Street in the 1960s, before its elimination.

2. In all of Memphis there is probably no greater body of knowledge about how it really was on Beale Street than Thomas Pinkston, second fiddle in W. C. Handy's band, pit player at the old Palace Theater. Here he stands on his front porch with his family in the late 60s.

3. Lillie Mae Glover—also known as Memphis Ma Rainey—in her Sun Records heyday.

4. Elvis's return to Tupelo, Mississippi, September 26, 1956. There are people whom this day remains the high point of their lives.

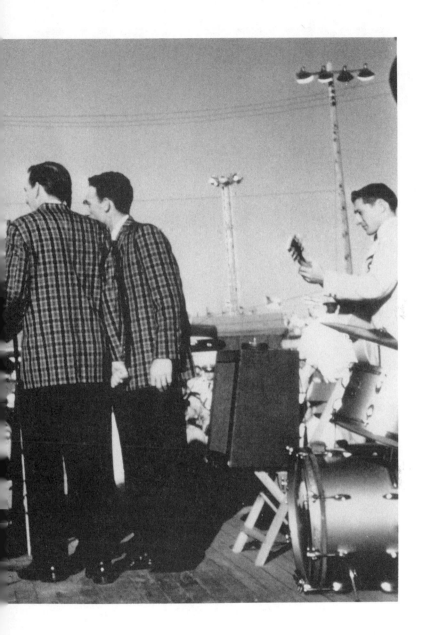

5. Probably because of his later country music success, Charlie Rich's contribution to rock's earliest stages tends to get overlooked.

6. Carl Perkins (center) remains one of the godfathers of early rockabilly.

7. Conway Twitty (second from left), a far cry from his later days as a country crooner. The girls used to go crazy.

8. Jerry Lee Lewis—the Killer—helped give early rock its manic, dangerous edges.

9. Johnny Cash, whose "Home of the Blues" is about the record store on Beale Street, poses with Elvis Presley.

10. Charlie Feathers hasn't changed much since his Sun Record days. Here he performs at the Beale Street Blues Festival in 1979.

11. Stax Records was named by and for its owners, Jim Stewart and Estelle Axton (STewart + AXton). Here Estelle proudly displays Sam & Dave's "Soul Man" in the Stax studio, 1968.

12.   Otis Redding defined '60s soul music.

13. Isaac Hayes (at the piano) and David Porter wrote some of Stax's most memorable material.

14. James Luther Dickinson, "Captain Memphis."

SUNSET

It was just like the day Jesus walked on earth—that's the way that music was. It just had to happen, because ... it ... it just had to happen. That's all ...
— Sun artist Charlie Feathers

So he got down on his knees before me and began to recite whole pages from the script. Elvis must have seen Rebel Without a Cause *a dozen times by then and remembered every one of Jimmy's (James Dean) lines.*
— Nicholas Ray, director of *Rebel Without a Cause*, on his meeting with Elvis Presley

There is a small green shingle-and-brick house in east Memphis. Inside, the walls are paneled in dark ersatz wood, the carpet is brown, and there is a green couch. On a large bureau is a stereo set, one of the kinds with a turntable, tape decks, AM/FM radio, and probably a four-speed transmission with overdrive built into it, and two records: *Charlie Feathers Volume One* and *Charlie Feathers Volume Two.* The man who made those two records is sitting next to me on the green couch, trying not to be bitter.

Charlie Feathers has a right to feel bitter because when history started sniffing around 706 Union Avenue, it pretty much managed to overlook Charlie. This is what he says about it:

"I recorded 'Tongue-Tied Jill,' which was a rockabilly record, for the first time in 1949. Nobody could understand that kind of music then, so nothing happened.

"I recorded several things with Scotty [Moore] and Bill [Black], who went on to play with Elvis, but we couldn't get it to come through the board.

"I'd be in the control room with Sam [Phillips] and be telling him what to do, and he'd take a lot of credit for it.

"I recorded some stuff on Elvis at a radio station in Helena, Arkansas, in 1955, and boy, was it hot stuff!

"I arranged Elvis' 'Mystery Train' and a bunch of other stuff, and of course I wrote the flip side of 'Mystery Train' myself.

"Jerry Lee Lewis got the idea for that pumping piano from me.

"People try to get that Sun Sound now, and they can't do it. I know how we got it . . . I say 'we,' I mean Sam. Sam owned it all.

"The secret of the Sun Sound, I know it. I know it well."

The secret of the Sun Sound.

Every city in this country has its little secret that its inhabitants seem to adopt as their own, almost on an instinctive level. In New York City it used to be that everybody was an actor, albeit unemployed. Nowadays

it's that everybody is a rock star, or going to be one by
tomorrow afternoon at the latest. Bump into somebody
on the street, ask what's up, and you'll get a rundown on
the new band. It's funny, in fact, how many of those little
secrets have to do with music, as if when we close our
eyes to dream, we arrange to do so in ten cuts that, with
overdubs, will make a dandy album. In Nashville everybody's secret is that everybody writes country music, and
the worst thing in the world that can happen is to be
trapped at somebody's house while he reads you a few
dozen of his favorites (the same is true in San Francisco,
where seemingly normal people have an unaccountable
urge to break into song at the drop of a hat).

In Memphis, ever out of step with the rest of the
planet, the secret is that everybody knows the secret of
Sun Records and, by default, Elvis Presley. Finding
somebody in Memphis who didn't have some vague, tan-
gential connection with Sun is like finding an ex-hippie
corporate vice-president who wasn't at Woodstock.

Actually, Charlie Feathers knows *two* secrets about Sun
Records. The first is the slap bass. The second is the
placement of the microphones.

"Rockabilly," says Charlie Feathers from across the
green couch, "has got to sound *thin*, or it's not really
rockabilly. See, rockabilly was the greatest music that
ever was. Some people's whole life was wrapped up in it.
But it's gotta sound thin, you know, just like it was getting ready to jump off the record at ya. That's the
secret."

Charlie Feathers' whole life is wrapped up in rockabilly, what happened in Memphis in the dim dark days
of the 1950s. Like so many others in our tale, he grew up
listening to the two pillars of southern music—black mu-

sic from the field and country music from the radio. He
wanted to play bluegrass, à la Bill Monroe, whom he
idolized, except bluegrass was complicated and there
wasn't anybody around to teach it to him. The closest
thing to a teacher he could find was a black sharecropper
named Junior Kimbro. So Charlie Feathers tried to sing
like Bill Monroe—that high, lonesome hillbilly wail—
while playing the guitar like a black sharecropper, slap-
ping the side of the instrument with gusto. But the music
life was hard, and soon Charlie Feathers was bumming
around the country, working in the oil fields of Texas,
driving a truck, working his way back to his hometown of
Holly Springs, Mississippi. By the late 1940s he'd arrived
in West Memphis, Arkansas, across the river from Memphis, where he happened onto Howlin' Wolf. His musical
fires rekindled, Charlie Feathers began hanging around
Sun Records almost from the day of its birth.

He worked with Sam Phillips in the studio, did odd
jobs and the like, but failed to touch the lodestone. The
music that Phillips heard in his head, the bastard fusion
of black and white, just wasn't what Charlie Feathers
was singing—although nobody doubted that it was *close*.
As to his claims, writer Peter Guralnick spent some time
in Memphis trying to sort out the truth from the myth.
After extensive interviews and fact checking, the best answer he could come up with was "maybe." Recently a
musicologist from Pennsylvania called me in the middle
of the night to ask me if, in my considered opinion, Charlie Feathers did indeed record Elvis Presley at a radio
station in Helena, Arkansas, in 1955. The only answer I
could give him was that Charlie said he did, and Elvis
was dead.

"Rockabilly was natural—it's like when you want a

drink of water, you go get a drink of water. Nothing else
will do," says Charlie Feathers. "There's a lot of fake to
the music nowadays. you either sing the song or you back
up and leave it alone. Elvis was like that because he sang
hard. The Beatles, they were just humming."

In his quiet little house in east Memphis Charlie
Feathers does indeed know a secret, but it has nothing to
do with the use of slap bass or the placement of microphones at Sam Phillips' studio.

He gives the secret away when he talks about men who
lived for rockabilly, because that is really the bottom
line. Like the blues, rockabilly sprang up organically,
across the South. And again like the blues, it wasn't until
the music came to Memphis, to be focused through the
lens of Sun Records and Sam Phillips, that it ignited a
revolution.

Sam Phillips has been quoted a million times as saying
that what he was looking for was a white boy who could
sing the blues. A redneck who acted like a Negro. A
country singer who could sing rhythm and blues. A white
nigger. He almost found him in Harmonica Frank Floyd,
the white hobo singer. And he really got close with Charlie Feathers, but his voice was still a little *too* hillbilly.

But is it so simple? Bill Haley and Pat Boone could
sing the blues, and at least one of that pair could rock.
White acts "covering" black music, as we've seen in earlier chapters, were as American as apple pie, and just
about as widespread. Many white men have sung the
blues; many will go on singing them.

But rockabilly, at its very bottom, is *mean* music, sung
through clenched teeth by red-eyed men who look as if
they've seen the wrong end of too many broken bottles.
That's something we've lost sight of today. We talk about

rockabilly as bright, upbeat, and fun music, and we search for "previously unissued" rockabilly records like a chicken scratching for the last bit of corn.

It's easy to forget that beneath the insipid lyrics and the simple rhythms, rockabilly tapped a wellspring of revolution. It dipped below the calm surface of the 1950s to the dark, smoldering potential of a generation looking for a voice. It's different today—every new musical trend (and there are at least a couple each week, it seems) previews some kind of "revolution." In the 1960s we sang songs about smashing the state and marching in the street, and in the 1970s we sang songs abut doing *something* before we all died of boredom. Since those days in the early 1950s we've sung the battle cries of a thousand different wars, and in our spiritual exhaustion we reach back to "happier" times when "grease" was the *word*, when music was "fun" and "light" and "exuberant." With a few decades safely between us and the music, we can manage to overlook the level of violence inherent in it, the shattering of a way of life.

Yet the violence walked hand in hand with an overwhelming sense of joy and release. Rockabilly is a statement of identity and a call to battle at the same time—I AM, the music says, OR ELSE. Which is why "Mystery Train," a song critic Nick Tosches once aptly described as a "demonic incantation," can still raise the hackles on the back of your neck after almost thirty years. And even the shoddiest of Christians can tell you that, yes, you can be released, but there will be a slight toll.

To the kids around Memphis, rockabilly was a revolution deeper and more profound than anything that would happen in the 1960s. You can still see a hint of that feeling in the faraway eyes of people like Carl Perkins and Jack Clement and Conway Twitty and Billy Lee

Riley when they talk about those nights twenty-five years
ago, when they walked out on stage knowing a grand
total of one or two or three songs, following Elvis or the
other way around, knowing that they'd have to reach
down deep inside them, inside their *souls,* and tap the
fires burning there to set the crowd on fire. And somewhere in their eyes you see the flush of victory as the
crowds came alive and their minds filled with the knowledge—the absolute stone-cold knowledge—that they were
changing the world.

Black music or white music, you take your pick. You
name your poison. But in Memphis—*Memphis* of all
places!—a whole bunch of people picked the wrong color.
A bunch of rednecks caught black music the way some
people get the gospel, and it was like finding a missing
piece of the puzzle, a missing piece of themselves.

When Elvis walked down Beale Street, he found a
missing piece of himself. When Carl Perkins first went to
the all-black Baptist Church in Jackson, Tennessee, and
lounged around on the car outside; when Jerry Lee Lewis
peeked in the window of a black church in Ferriday,
Louisiana; when Conway Twitty listened to his first field
hand singing the blues—they found missing pieces of
themselves, and they went to Memphis to try and make
other people understand their vision.

What happened in Memphis in the days that followed
a certain July afternoon in 1954 was that for a second or
two, black and white understood each other completely,
on a gut level, and the world rocked.

That is what Charlie Feathers understands so completely that he doesn't even see a need to verbalize it. In a
sense, Charlie Feathers hasn't changed since those early
days at Sun—the same can be said of many of the other

Sun artists and even fans. The fusing of black and white was and is a heady brew, one not soon forgotten, and we are forced to fall back on the church for the only explanation that holds even a little water. When people accept what the church—specifically the fundamentalist Christian religion that permeates the life of the South (Memphis boasts more churches than any other city of its size in the country)—believes, they look at the world through different eyes. The events may be the same as they were before, but the perception of them isn't. Such is being "born again."

What happened in Memphis was a secular religious revival; the slate was washed clean and the disciples could never again see the world in quite the same way.

Like many others who touched the Sun tower, Conway Twitty, *née* Harold Jenkins (he took his performing name from the towns of Conway, Arkansas, and Twitty, Texas), has found fame, fortune, and a permanent home in country music, and those dim days of the 1950s might as well belong to another person on another planet, right?

Wrong.

Like so many others, Twitty grew up in the Mississippi Delta, listening to the twin poles of the black blues next door and the Grand Ole Opry on the radio. "So I grew up playing some kind of combination between the blues and country," he says. "It was really inevitable. Every country musician today has been subjected to the blues."

For him, there was really no other choice. "It was like there was a magnifying glass over Memphis," he says. "It was bigger than life." Especially after young Harold Jenkins heard his first Elvis Presley record in March of 1956. "I thought, 'Boy, I've heard that before!' It was just a mix of country and blues, and even though I knew I wasn't good enough to sing real country music, I knew I could sing that Elvis stuff." Sometimes, he laughs, Harold Jenkins would spend twelve hours in the little studio at 706 Union Avenue, looking for the flash of fire that would fuse black and white. "That was the great thing about the place," he remembers. "Sam would let just anybody come in and do it."

After the recording, he'd hit the road with the other members of the Sun troupe—Carl Perkins, who'd been playing that bastard country-blues mix for years in the ratty clubs around Jackson, Tennessee; Johnny Cash, who wanted to be a country singer; Roy Orbison, the man with the incredible voice and the mean guitar; and sometimes even the greatest of them all, Elvis Presley.

"This was really the great part of it," he says, and his enthusiasm gives him away: the country crooner still believes. "We all played the same little ole places—schoolhouses, clubs, places like Truman, Arkansas, and Maudlin, Missouri—and Elvis had a couple of hit songs, and Carl had a couple. We all had a few records to pull stuff from, but the music was brand new. Once you got past those records, you just had to create something. You had two or three songs you could memorize, but after that, it was all up to you. And once in a while someone out there on that stage created something, and we'd all pick up on it. It was like reaching out and pulling something out of nothing, and it felt great."

Of course, Conway Twitty did go on to that proverbial fame and fortune, beginning in 1959 with a song called "It's Only Make Believe," which he wrote at the Flamingo Lounge in Ontario, Canada. But the first wave passed ("You wanna know what happened to rockabilly?" singer Billy Swan, who rode the top of the charts with a rockabilly-tinted song called "I Can Help," asked me late one night in Atlanta. "The record companies couldn't handle it, so they just shut it out. It never died, you just couldn't hear it anymore."), and Conway Twitty decided that he was ready to be a country singer. That proved to be tough. Country music had taken a vicious beating from the Memphis wild men, so vicious that many people in Nashville were deathly afraid that "traditional" country music would cease to exist. When the fires were banked, Nashville was hardly ready to open its arms to the rock and roll refugees. But Conway Twitty prevailed and is now something of a Nashville icon. When he recently decided to change his hairdo, banishing forever the 1950s pompadour that was so much a part of his style, he rated a whole article in *People* magazine, complete with "before" and "after" pictures.

But while the old fires may burn low, they never seem to burn out. One particular concert in Charlotte, North Carolina, after a major stock-car race, comes to mind. The bill featured Conway Twitty and Loretta Lynn, the show was as country as sorghum molasses, and the fifty thousand or so people in the stands loved every minute of it. Most of them were on the far side of thirty and not unaccustomed to working with their hands. After Loretta Lynn, Conway Twitty took the stage and launched into his greatest hits, his smooth voice describing numerous hidden places on numerous trembling young virgins. But he seemed slightly off balance, not quite feeling the songs he sung. When he finished, he stopped his band, the Twittybirds, and made a speech. I am, he explained, country to the core. Conway Twitty talked about what country music meant to him, how important it was, blah, blah. When he finished, he got a standing ovation. He stood quietly for a minute, then he signaled his band to follow him.

And he rocked. For the next thirty minutes he ripped across the stage like a wild man, his eyes glazed, his slicked-back pompadour in a shambles, howling out rockabilly madness like there was not going to be any tomorrow.

And the crowd went absolutely stark-raving *mad*, shouting and screaming and running at the stage; forgetting the patient homilies they'd been telling their children only that afternoon; forgetting their deadly jobs at service stations and banks; forgetting the dishes, the mortgage payments; the shattered dreams that crunched underfoot like so much broken china—they *rocked*.

From our spot in front of the stage, my friend whistled softly. We'd just returned from a whirlwind tour of most of the South doing research for his book. We had talked to some of the biggest names in country and rock, seen dozens of shows from stadiums to honky-tonks, and were feeling pretty jaded. Until we looked into the wild eyes of the 1950s, only a few feet away.

"Good Lord," my friend said, with a mixture of awe and fear.

And then it was over, a thrown switch. Conway Twitty smoothed his hair; the crowd glanced nervously to its side to see if anyone had noticed. The air was still, as if a UFO had just landed and taken off and nobody could quite remember what it looked like.

We always knew what we had, says Judd Phillips, Sam's older brother and partner in the Sun enterprise. "It was the poor white seeking the soul expression. Not the uptown white, but the poor white. But the Negro could not be accepted as an *idol;* it was a *sin.* But what happened, all of this explosion, was because of the poor black trash and the poor white trash, and the only reason it happened in Memphis was that nobody cared here."

ROCK AND ROLL
IN BETWEEN

Popular art depicts the world not as it is, nor even as it might be, but as we would have it.

—Dr. Abraham Kaplan,
The Popular Arts: A Critical Reader

Nostalgia is a falsification of the good old days. There were no good old days.

—Eleanora Foa,
The New York Times

By the late 1950s rock and roll had entered the Horse Latitudes, bobbing almost motionlessly on an unending ocean of stagnation. The brightest lights were already extinguished, and the new flames from across the ocean were barely burning yet. It is the heartland of Nostalgia, where right was Right and wrong was Wrong and all the cheerleaders virtuous. It was in the midst of this stagnation that rock and roll was transformed from a fad into

127

an industry, and adopted a tone it still maintains today. One might even be tempted to say that rock grew up, except that would imply it is grown up today.

Perhaps the most important thing that happened in the period between the fading of Elvis and the rise of the Beatles was that the rock singer accepted the mantle of godhood and the music assumed its status as a mythic event. The old covenant between the singer and the audience, hammered out through many years on the road by traveling singers both black and white, was broken. In its place was a Celebrity and an Event.

Country music singer Ernest Tubb once described the way he sang as "being so simple that any boy out there in the field who hears it will think, 'Heck, I can do that!' " While the traveling singers of the 1930s and 1940s were seen as slightly disreputable outcasts, they were nonetheless recognized as important members of the community, an organic part of the fabric of everyday life, though their lifestyles were certainly no great shakes. The importance of a hillbilly singer or bluesman or gospel singer lay in the relationship between the singer and the audience. The singer provided a service—making life easier to bear—for which he received a little bit of money, a warm place to sleep, and more than his share of the local womanhood—at least to hear it told.

This nonspectacular relationship was so deeply rooted that modern researchers have had a tough time establishing what it was *really* like back then. "Nobody paid any attention to who was onstage," said Hank Williams' researcher Chet Flippo. "They came to dance."

"I've talked to dozens of people who listened to the blues greats—people like Robert Johnson—about the honky-tonks," said one well-known blues' researcher. "What was going on," I asked, "were people dancing, did they listen to the lyrics? And they usually just look at me like I was crazy. Sometimes I think they just tell me what I want to hear."

The first time Elvis went tooling down the street in his pink Cadillac all that changed. Elvis was more than simply an extension of his audience. He was a figurehead for that audience, a living, breathing symbol of the revolution that all the kids of the 1950s were beginning to feel. He had come from the community—his was a genuine country-fried rags-to-riches tale that is no less poignant for being true—but he was no longer part of the community and he never would be again. Instead, he adopted the trappings of the aristocracy America had never had and always wanted. (Remember Richard Nixon's Louis XIV costumes for his White House guards a few years ago?) He became a superstar.

But Elvis couldn't become a superstar for all the people—not yet. He was too close to his roots in the rural South, too close to that pimply-faced, swivel-hipped kid who sang the Devil's music. So Colonel Tom Parker set about on his infamous campaign to turn Elvis from a rockabilly rebel into a pussycat lounge singer. His ultimate success closed the door on the first rock moment and opened the door to the future.

Which is where we came in at the beginning of this chapter. Rock and roll in the late 1950s and early 1960s marked the beginning of a shift from the specific—the hard-nosed rebels—to the general—the rock and roll band. The late 1950s mark the beginning of the rock and roll mythology, the gospel according to rock.

Not everybody was thrilled about rock's impending deification. Parents took it especially hard, as this quote from a magazine of the times shows:

"Every once in a while, half the kids in the country seem to go wild over some sulky, sideburned, guitar-twanger in a zooty suit," wrote one distressed parent in 1959. "Give a girl a good home, every advantage, a careful upbringing, and she sneaks home pictures of a calf-eyed no-account singer she wouldn't dare bring in the front door." And this was a report urging moderation! The rest is equally informative: "It's primitive and brutal, just thump-thump-thump, honking sax and demented wails from people with names like the Teddy Bears or the Five Blops. Its tastelessness aside, you can't help feeling that this is the music of cheap night spots, tawdry roadhouses, drunk, delinquent, often enough with leering sexual innuendo. The kids love it like a narcotic, too, you have noticed.

"Certainly the music is bad enough. Monotonous and unmelodic, it is about as musical as a concrete mixer with rocks in the hopper. The vocalizing is so agonized, you can barely make out the words. But what little you can comprehend doesn't exactly put your mind at ease. 'Lyrics,' they call them. Hah!"

Whisper magazine in 1959 didn't pull any punches:

"She was a 16-year-old girl. Clinical tests confirmed that she was an active VD carrier. Quizzed about her contacts with men, she broke down and told a remarkable story.

"A week before she had gone to a rock 'n' roll session at a local 'clubhouse.' The boys got her drunk, kept her drunk for several days. *During this period 41 men and boys lined up and had sexual contact with her, one after the other!* [their italics]."

After much hand wringing and soul searching, the Massachusetts Department of Public Health put its finger on the source of the scourge (at least according to *Whisper*): *the rock and roll craze that is sweeping the country!*

"Certain types of rock 'n' roll—those with filthy lyrics, exploited by greedy vendors and disc jockeys with peg pants and d.a. haircuts—contribute to the emotional frenzy and sexual promiscuity of teenagers.

"He [Dr. Nicholas J. Fiumara, director of the VD clinic] called attention to the 'peculiar, almost hypnotic effect of this oft-repeated beat' of this type of music, and to the 'sexually suggestive body motions' of rock and roll dancing. Such parties often turn into an orgy of heavy drinking and wild necking, with many young couples adjourning to parked cars for further intimacies."

Hard to believe, but it actually gets better, describing in great detail the lurid sexual activities perpetrated by rock-crazed sex fiends. After reading this article I was afraid to touch a jukebox for weeks without disinfecting my hands afterward. The strange fact is that they were basically *right,* rock and roll really did all those things. Boys and girls got together; blacks and whites joined hands, just like the poster promulgated by the United Klans of America threatened they would. Young America drank whiskey, smoked the weed formerly relegated to the backwaters of jazz musicians, got together and talked in a *cr-aaaaaaaazy* language. Kids dressed funny and talked funny and danced funny and thought funny ideas.

By golly, the grown-ups were right—rock and roll *did* represent a clear and present threat to the existing social order.

Myth is a generalized superstructure that we use to help slot ourselves into everyday life. Older societies had myths about dragons and knights and gods fighting on the tops of mountains. The New World adopted a more prosaic mythology, peopled with hard-boiled detectives who never take bribes, Cowboys and Indians, Woodstock Nation, G-men, the Kennedy Family, and . . . Rock and Roll. For a long time the most pervasive myth in America was the one about Cowboys and Indians. All those personal traits we found admirable we grafted onto the guys with the white hats, until we got embarrassed about killing off the competition. Then we changed sides, letting the Indians come out in the white hats for a change.

Today's myth is about rock and roll musicians who live in a magic world filled with celebrities, fawning fans, truckloads of money, and lots of neat drugs that will alter your brain and cause you to go to Mexico to get your nose replaced with a new Plexiglas model impervious to weird chemicals. If you are a rock and roll musician, you are temporarily exempted from the normal laws of cause and effect. Unless, of course, you are black, in which case just when you think you've got your exemption, the Man shows up with a surprise . . . as in 1979, when Chuck Berry found himself back in prison on an income tax evasion rap. During the trial it became plain that the "evasion" was more in the nature of an oversight and that full restitution would be made. No dice, said the judge, who realized that nothing is lower than a creature of myth whose magic has forsaken him. Put him away. A few months before, Rolling Stone Keith Richard had walked away from a heroin bust in Canada with some nitwit sentence about performing for the needy. His mojo was still working, and he was the right color.

The next few chapters are about how things got to be that way and how it hurt the music.

In *Counter-Clock World*, a science-fiction novel by Philip

K. Dick, everyone grows younger. Not in a mental sense, but in a real physical way—one starts out an old person and ends up a baby instead of vice versa. All in all, not a bad deal. Instead of ending up a dottering old man, the neighborhood embarrassment, one ends up a cutesy, cuddly baby.

That's the way rock and roll has always worked. At its birth, it was a dirty old man, making leering comments at the ladies and rubbing a huge bulge in its pants. It soon developed acne, a thirst for fast cars and 3.2 percent beer, and a reverent attachment to itsy-bitsy teeny-weeny bikinis. Then rock began growing up again, to ponder the mysteries of the universe, life, and growing up, only to begin the cycle again.

Rhythm and blues and the blues were (and are) grown-up music. The themes they deal with and the manner in which they deal with them are hardly childish—one of the reasons, maybe even the main reason, they never achieved the national popularity of rock. The classic examples are Hank Ballard's "Work with Me Annie" series, and they're not talking about the office. In most of black music the sensual is pretty well integrated with the culture itself, which is not surprising given the emotional nature of the African culture on which the music is based. To use one of the great clichés of the 1970s, the Africans were "in touch with each other and in touch with the earth." Not to be in touch with people and surroundings meant ending up one afternoon as dinner for an angling crocodile. The omnipresence of dance in early black culture also led white observers (who were reasonably sure that if you weren't in church worrying about your everlasting soul, you were figuring a way to damn it to everlasting hellfire) to believe that the dancing was part of some bizarre sexual rite. In some cases, of course, they were right.

In Hermann Hesse's *Steppenwolf* Harry Haller has been drawn to a jazz dance hall. Haller is both drawn to the music, comparing it to the steam of raw flesh, and repulsed by it, since the music makes his body—rather than his mind—wiggle. In the Southern Baptist Church dancing was considered only slightly less sinful than drinking bootleg whiskey and making a pass at your mother. To dance was to join hands—join bodies, actually—with a spirit older than Christianity, and that spirit was irredeemably evil in its nature.

Thus to have the popular potential, the music had to get younger, to appeal to kids just entering their teens along with the 1960s. The first rock and roll madmen— Elvis Presley, Buddy Holly, Carl Perkins, Jerry Lee Lewis—weren't the answer, for they were *still* too old, the emotions displayed in their songs too complex and revolutionary. "Hound Dog" might be damned as silly and trite by the parents of America, but there were in-group implications throughout the song that really scared them shitless. It was an "us versus them" song; the kids knew it, and so, at heart, did their parents. Rockabilly was diamond-hard music tied to the real life of the streets. Every time Jerry Lee Lewis opened his mouth, three more girls in Cincinnati, Ohio, inexplicably got pregnant; Chuck Berry sounded as if he was making fun, maybe inviting your daughter over for a quick romp. No siree, rock and roll was still too *old*, too experienced for its own good.

So it got younger.

The trick was explained very nicely by Nat Hentoff in *Esquire* magazine in 1961, near the end of rock's transition period. *Esquire* was quite worried about the state of popular music, which was refusing to turn toward the more intellectual jazz the magazine favored. "The grindingly mediocre level of most pop music—and pop singers," wrote Hentoff, "is due essentially not to the existence of a little mafia in the music business, but to what teenagers—the basic consumers of pop music—*do* want.

"It's not surprising then that so many pop song hits shake with such formalized frenzy, emotions that cannot be directly expressed, that cannot be fulfilled, because frustration and daydreaming are preferable for most of the young to taking a chance, to being unique, let alone uniquely wrong."

At the time that article was written, the top song in the country was Elvis Presley's "Stuck on You," one of his poorest efforts. Elvis had just nudged out Percy Faith's "Theme from A Summer Place," and already the Everly Brothers' superslick "Cathy's Clown" and Connie Francis' "Everybody's Somebody's Fool" were shooting up the charts. In fact, the only ringer in sight was the Hollywood Argyles' "Alley-Oop." One wonders why the article was even written. The only apparent danger from popular music was death by boredom.

Perhaps more telling is a later quote from songwriter Jerry Leiber, who, along with Mike Stoller, practically revolutionized popular music in the late 1950s and early 1960s. Rock and roll, he said, is "a means of escape from reality. We write the lyrics deliberately vague. The songs aren't addressed to anybody real, but to dream characters. The songs are egocentric and dreamy. Lots of basic blues ideas wouldn't wash as rock and roll lyrics because the blues are too real, too earthy. You have to make them more dreamlike and very moral. That's why you're rarely going to hear even a plain *happy* rock and roll song, because happiness is a real emotion."

Jerry Leiber and Mike Stoller are two of the stranger cases of white boys who, in this case, wrote the blues. Leiber was born in Baltimore, Stoller in California, but both grew up in California. The older Stoller was already in college when he ran into Jerry Leiber, who had been writing songs for a couple of years.

These two young white kids, California kids at that, wanted to grow up to be songwriters. They wanted to write the blues, which had about as much to do with white kids in California as the next moon shot. Leiber sang the blues songs they wrote in a record store where he worked and was heard by Leonard Sill of Modern Records, one of the kingpins of the rhythm and blues scene in southern California. Sill was impressed enough to get the kids an appointment with his bosses, the Bihari brothers, who, along with Leonard Chess in Chicago and Sam Phillips in Memphis, controlled the rhythm and blues world. "After we had waited about twenty minutes past the time of our appointment," Stoller told Charlie Gillett in *Making Tracks,* "we got very upset and walked out. Just down the street was Aladdin Records, so we went in there and they bought two of our songs."

The songs clicked, and within a couple of years Leiber and Stoller were hot writing properties, managing to turn out two classics—"K.C. Lovin', " better known to the world as "Kansas City," and "Hound Dog," which remains one of the best-known songs in the history of rock and roll.

If you can listen to either song and figure out how they were written by two white kids just spittin' distance out of high school, you're one step beyond me. The incredi-

ble thing about the early music of Leiber and Stoller was
that it was so . . . well, *real;* earthy, the very thing they
would have to watch out for in the future. They talked
about them mean streets with the easy grace of someone
who's been there so many times that it's totally second
nature to him now—just step over the drunks, sir, and
don't mind the razor.

After the stupendous success of "Hound Dog" (and a
byzantine legal battle between the boys and bandleader
Johnny Otis as to who owned the song), Leiber and
Stoller went to work with their own group, the Robins, a
spinoff of Otis's group. While Elvis was singing the
praises of Dean Martin, Leiber was hoping to grow up to
be either Cole Porter or Irving Berlin. In the meantime,
he was working on such rhythm and blues classics as
"Riot in Cell Block #9" (for the Robins); "Hound Dog"
(for Willie Mae Thornton); "Jailhouse Rock" (for Elvis
Presley); "Young Blood" backed with "Searchin' " (for
the Coasters), two of the greatest party records ever written; "Yakety Yak," "Charlie Brown," "Poison Ivy,"
"Wake Me Shake Me," "Little Egypt" (all for the Coasters); and god knows what else.

From there, Leiber and Stoller went on to provide material for the Drifters ("There Goes My Baby") and to
work with other songwriters such as Carole King and
Gerry Goffin (who wrote all the *rest* of the songs you
remember from that era). Here's where things get tricky
in much the same way things get tricky when we start
dealing with the rockabilly wild men in Memphis. The
temptation is to say that Leiber and Stoller, two of the
more important influences on pop music in the late
1950s, swiped their moves from blacks, just like that,
thank you. White bandleader Johnny Otis—another

strange case—remembers helping the two white kids with the argot of the ghetto. "They would bring songs and I would help rewrite them," Otis told Charlie Gillett for *Making Tracks.* "For instance, once they had a song that had razor-cuttin' and gin-drinkin' and dice-shootin', and they didn't understand this was derogatory to black people. They were just young guys who meant well, they weren't racist in the true sense of the word."

"Actually, the more intelligent the white, the more the realization he has to steal from niggers," wrote LeRoi Jones in *Black Music* in 1966. "They take from us all the way down the line. Finally, what's the difference between the Beatles and the Stones etc., and Minstrelsy? Minstrels never convinced anybody they were black either."

There has been a strong liberal trend in popular music in recent years to ratify Jones's claims across the board and deliver the entire history of American folk music into the black tradition. Like the late-date bopper in this book's introduction—cruising down Fourteenth Street with his icebox-sized radio and alien beat—popular culture again has gone whole hog in the wrong direction, refusing to see that the advances in the music have come from the clash between black and white. Leiber and Stoller didn't "steal" rhythm and blues songs. Rather, they added a distinct white-kid-growing-up-in-California element to them. They "popified" the songs, made them younger, and hence more acceptable to the budding rock audience. By making them younger and, ultimately, less worldly, they made the songs a little whiter as well, which, in turn, opened the music to a much larger audience waiting in the wings; an audience that was thrashing around searching for the common denominator: the hummable tune.

So, as Jerry Leiber wrote, the search for that tune takes place in the strangest of places, a childhood we wish was ours. We cry because "Smoke Gets in Your Eyes" (No. 1 hit, January 1959), we search for a "Venus" (March 1959), we agonize at being a "Lonely Boy" (July 1959), "Mr. Blue" (November 1959), "Cathy's Clown" (May 1960), a "Soldier Boy" (May 1962), or, if we're really slick, a "Travelin' Man" (May 1961). We worry that "It's Only Make Believe" (November 1958), that she won't "Save the Last Dance for Me" (October 1960), that "Everybody's Somebody's Fool" (June 1960). We cry because somebody swiped our boyfriend when we were just building up the nerve to kiss him (or at least wear his ring). We understand something that even the very best bluesman had trouble with, the nature of love. We can fall in love at a glance, race back to a doomed car to recapture a high school ring, wonder whether the angels up above are jealously watching our love.

We are, in short, younger, and with the passing of the big guns—Elvis in the Army and on his way to becoming straight; Buddy Holly dead; Bill Haley scared of his own success; Carl Perkins, Gene Vinson, and all the other greats fallen victim to their very greatness—we begin to wallow in the world as we think we see it, as we might mold it and shape it with our adolescent minds. It is Camelot, and as in the Jazz Age, all things are possible.

SMILING THROUGH
THE SIXTIES

The 1960s have been edited, lost in a permanent wave of nostalgia, and dulled at all the edges by a constant re-stamping of the die. Grasping the 1960s is like reaching back into a long-running version of George Lucas's 1973 film, *American Graffiti,* with a whole cast of soon-to-be-famous actors cluttering up our psychic closets.

November 22, 1963 stands out in the early part of the decade; John F. Kennedy was shot in Dallas and everything changed. If there is any single event from those days riveted to our psyches, it's that fusillade in Dallas. It forms a convenient demarcation, a Mason-Dixon line between the Old Days, sometimes referred to as "good," and the New Times, variously tagged as hard, cold, violent, and self-absorbed.

When John F. Kennedy died, "Deep Purple," by Nino Tempo and April Stevens, was the top song in the country, entering its second week at the head of the charts. In a few weeks the charts and the country would be captivated by the Singing Nun trilling "Dominique" and strumming her guitar. Within three months an unknown group from Liverpool, England, fresh from their huge British success with "She Loves You," would change the world with a song called "I Want to Hold Your Hand." The transition days of rock's adolescence would be over.

The early 1960s, though, were a critical time for rock and roll. During that period rock came to grips with whether it would continue rolling along or die the ignominious death of just another fad. The early rock of the 1950s was powered by fury, fueled by a generation exhilarated at finding its voice. We look back on the violent reaction to the first rock with humor, and even our parents are prone to blushing when we point out a sermon, a newspaper article, an off-hand comment on rock from the 1950s: "His gyrations, his nose-wiping, his leers are vulgar," wrote *Look* magazine in 1956 about Elvis Presley. "When asked about the sex element in his act, he answers without blinking his big brown eyes, 'Ah don't see anything wrong with it. Ah just act the way ah feel.' But Elvis will also grin and say, 'Without my left leg, ah'd be dead.' " But by 1960 rock was getting ready to establish itself permanently and make a quantum sexual leap forward on the hips of a star-struck kid from Philadelphia.

The year opened with Marty Robbins' "El Paso," drifted through "Running Bear" and "Itsy Bitsy Teenie Weenie Yellow Polka Dot Bikini" and "Theme from A Summer Place," with the new, sanitized Elvis contributing "Stuck on You," "It's Now or Never," and "Are You Lonesome Tonight?" In all respects but one it was a mellow year, to borrow a bit of terminology from the seventies, meaning *boring*.

The exception had to do with a Philadelphia boy

named Ernest Evans, who while still in high school had the unlikely job of chicken plucker at the local poultry house. When he wasn't plucking chickens, he was regaling the customers with his renditions of popular songs and his lively sense of humor. Henry Colt, who owned the shop, thought Ernest had a lot of talent and should be doing something with his life other than separating chickens from their feathers, so he went to Kal Mann, an acquaintance who also happened to be a songwriter, and delivered one of the great lines from the entertainment business: "Give this kid a listen, and see what you think. Just give him a break."

Mann was impressed enough to sign Ernest to a long-term contract (another hoary music business tradition) with Cameo-Parkway Records, a Philadelphia label already doing quite well with Bobby "Volare" Rydell. But what can you do with a kid named Ernest Evans? Sounds like a winner at the science fair. Besides, one of the greatest show-business traditions of all was that you don't have to use your real name, even if there's nothing wrong with it. Remember that Shelly Fabares legally changed her name from *Michelle* Fabares. . . . The problem was solved by Mrs. Dick Clark, who happened to see Ernest on her husband's television show. Since Ernest idolized Fats Domino, why not call him Chubby? And, come to think of it, why not a play on "Domino" as well? Why not call him Chubby Checker?

With contract in hand, all the newly christened Chubby needed was a song. The first came in 1959, a modest hit written by Mann called "The Class." Okay, but not a world-shaker, and Cameo-Parkway was definitely looking for a world-shaker. Unlike most other companies, they were in the perfect position to pull it off.

They were in Philadelphia, and so was Dick Clark and his *American Bandstand,* a show launched on ABC television in 1957 that was the very soul of simplicity—play music, and a bunch of kids get up and dance. By 1960 the show was an established tastemaker, having weathered falling record sales and payola scandals to occupy a special place in the hearts of teenagers. For all intents and purposes, *American Bandstand* was the arbiter of rock taste, and television wasn't interested in that bad-ass stuff.

But *Bandstand* sure could use a good dance, and Chubby Checker sure could use a good song.

An old-time black rhythm and blues group called Hank Ballard and the Midnighters provided them with both. Hank Ballard along with a lot of other R & B singers in the early 1950s, made a specialty of sexy music: explicit lyrics—to heck with the double entendre—and R & B dance music, perfectly suited to the sleazy clubs of Chicago, Cincinnati, Memphis, and every other major urban area. In 1954 Ballard plucked a line out of the floating body of blues lyrics that had been around since Day One and wrote his first "hit," "Work with Me Annie," which, in its last incarnation, had been "Roll with Me Henry." Apparently, Annie got worked pretty well, since the song was followed by "Annie Had a Baby" (written by Henry Glover of King Records). Both songs, along with another Ballard composition, "Sexy Ways," were million-sellers, although they were banned on most black radio stations for being too dirty—a pretty common occurrence throughout the 1950s. Most black groups were relegated to the R & B stations, but even they couldn't get away with too much.

But in 1959 Hank came up with a new dance step and the music to go along with it. No great shakes or innovation, more a codification of the shake-your-ass boogie that was the very soul of R & B. He put it on the flip side of a song he was excited about, "Teardrops on My Pillow," and released it on King Records in March of that year. It was the B-side that made it, a huge rhythm and blues hit called "The Twist." Sales were over a million—to a black audience, of course.

One year later Chubby Checker was in the studio recording a note-for-note cover of "The Twist," this time for white audiences, specifically for the Dick Clark show. It was a marriage made in heaven, and the Twist tore out of Philadelphia as a genuine, full-blown fad. All over the country, kids were thrusting out their posteriors, flexing their knees, and, for lack of a better word, "twisting" the night away, while record companies geared up with the likes of Gary U.S. Bonds, Joey Dee and the Starliters, Lee Dorsey, the Dovells, Bobby Lewis, the Miracles, and the Marvelettes.

Everybody, but *everybody*, was doing the Twist, from New York's sleazy Peppermint Lounge to Podunk High School in Nowhere, Indiana. More than one writer has scratched his head over the Twist. Even discounting the straight lift from Hank Ballard, it was not original. Ballard watched his audience, watched the way they moved, then copied it—a grand tradition in black music, and the very first tradition that white popular music *did* copy. Black dances were sort of like blues lyrics, ubiquitous and there for anybody who wanted to pick them up. It hardly seemed likely that one such dance should take the country by storm, hailed by some as important as the beginning of rock itself.

But it did, and the reason it did was simply a question of timing. Consider the year 1960 as an echo of the heyday period of the mid-1950s. From 1958 on, rock had fallen on hard times. That's hard to see through the *American Graffiti* filter; with our handily edited past, all we remember are the greatest hits. Songs that were only moderately successful when released—if, indeed, they were successful at all—are remembered as monster hits. The Isley Brothers' original "Twist and Shout" got to No. 17 on the charts; Charlie Rich's "Lonely Weekends" to No. 22; even the Marvelettes' "Please Mr. Postman" was No. 1 for only one short week. With our voracious appetite for nostalgia, we've sifted through the 1960s with a fine-toothed comb, and it's hard to separate the true phenomena from the chaff. But rock had fallen on hard times, and by the middle of 1960 it was about time for something, *anything,* to break the monotony, to flash back to the fury of the 1950s. That 1950s fury came from the almost religious fever of white boys singing black music.

Singing was not a strong enough word. Those boys had gotten the *gospel,* belief in the holy church of rhythm and blues, shake your bottom and sing like there's no tomorrow. Rip yourself apart, white boy, and *howl!* Not surprisingly, it couldn't go on forever. Nick Tosches, in *Country: The Biggest Music in America,* states flatly that by 1955 the initial white-boy rock explosion was finished. By the time it made the charts, it really wasn't there.

Like a hurting junkie, music needed a new shot of rhythm and blues, and along came Chubby Checker with a big needle. The great thing about Chubby Checker, at least from the *American Bandstand* point of view, was that he was *clean,* a product of the 1950s' rockers rather than the 1940s' electric bluesmen, and he didn't have any weird songs like "Work with Me Annie" lurking in the background, just waiting to erupt right in the middle of an all-girl audience. Not to worry, Mr. and Mrs. America, Chubby Checker isn't going to ravish your daughters! That he happened to be black was strictly a bonus. ("Listen," a friend tells me before a Chubby Checker show in New York City, these many years later, "be careful if you talk to Chubby. He doesn't like to get lumped in there with all them other niggers. I mean, he's not exactly a black singer, if you get my meaning.")

Rhythm and blues—once removed. That "once removed" is important, for what we're talking about here is sex, albeit well disguised. The Twist was the first overtly sexual dance for the Baby Boom kids to achieve the status of national mania. It was dirty. It was all movement, no steps; the body twisted and the bottom shook, and no matter how many times smiling faces on talk shows explained that it was just another dance, one quick cut to all those writhing bodies on the dance floor of the Peppermint Lounge was enough to shatter that illusion. It was a dance that could be mastered with little or no instruction in a couple of minutes, and it lent itself to personal—sometimes very personal—interpretation. The Twist took dancing out of the soda shop and put it in the streets, where people wiggled and sweated and thought unclean thoughts. In fact, the only reason the Twist got away with as much as it did was that the people doing it didn't *touch*. At least, not during the dance. "Remember slow dancing!" was the plaint of the waning generation, as the new generation twisted the night away to a black man singing a black song lifted from another black man. And maybe that's important in itself—Chubby Checker was one of the first black artists to gain total acceptance by the white audience. The black 1950s rock and rollers like Chuck Berry and Bo Diddley—even Little Richard—

occupied a strange place beyond the realm of color. They were neither black nor white, they were shouters. And they never suggested boys and girls get together and dance, either. But Checker did, and it worked.

"The Twist" was important for one other major reason: it represented the ascendancy of the rhythm, of the beat, over the song as a whole. The operative phrase became "Can you dance to it?" and, as usual when dance gains ascendancy, the music itself suffered. We're still sorting out that schism between music you dance to and music you listen to.

"The Twist" and the Twist shook America's complacency just as the Cuban missile crisis would soon shake the world's, but that was about its only significance. In itself, the Twist did little more than set the stage for the big changes coming in the later 1960s, for it, and the truckload of dance songs that followed, weren't strong enough to dig in and overcome the terrible lethargy of the times.

"As if the Mind had shouted to the Body, 'I'm ready!'—the Twist, superseding the Hula Hoop, burst upon the scene like a nuclear explosion, sending its fallout of rhythm into the Minds and Bodies of the people," wrote then Black Panther Eldridge Cleaver in his 1968 book *Soul on Ice*. "The Twist was a guided missile, launched from the ghetto into the very heart of suburbia. The Twist succeeded, as politics, religion, and law could never do, in writing in the heart and soul what the Supreme Court could only write in the books. The Twist was a form of therapy for a convalescing nation. . . . They were swinging and gyrating and shaking their dead little asses like petrified zombies trying to regain the warmth of life, rekindle the dead limbs, the cold ass, the stone heart, the stiff, mechanical, disused joints with the spark of life."

The Twist was the last preparation for the total ascension of rock and roll that would take place with the coming of the Beatles. The Twist became an acceptable alternative to wrestling in the back of Daddy's car, an alternative to grabbing a little paradise by the dashboard lights. The Twist made those dirty jungle rhythms acceptable—rumor had it that even Jackie and the Prez were twisting secretly in the Rose Garden. With the Twist, the last die was cast, and a whole generation of young people bided their time, waiting for the coming of the perfect wave from across the sea.

LIMEY ROCK

After the Beatles, the rock performer began to be seen not just as an entertainer but as a social visionary, archetypal citizen of a new society.

> —Lloyd Grossman, writing in
> *A Social History of Rock Music*

In the dead of winter at the end of January 1964 America was suffering through such a depression of the spirit that not even the most frantic twisting could cure it. Camelot had given way to the Great Society, the world was a troubled and cold place, and the best the radio could turn up was the Singing Nun and Bobby Vinton. America's teenagers were on the verge of a tremendous national sulk—outthrust chin, pouty cheeks, and all. Then, on the 25th of January, the Old World ended and the New World began. On that day the first Beatles song, "I Want to Hold Your Hand," entered the American charts. Within a week it was the top song in the country (knocked out seven weeks later by "She Loves You," also by the Beatles), being a teenager was all fun again, winter was giving way to an early spring, and what has come to be called the British Invasion was in full swing.

Quite simply, American kids went berserk for British music, a situation that held the charts enthralled until well into 1968, the golden year of rock and roll. Why the British Invasion happened is one of the perennial rock and roll questions that surface at least once in every serious discussion (or stoned ramble) about rock. The answers range from the most basic, given to me by a well-known rock critic who happened to be in England in 1963–1964—"It was different," he said, "and American kids were dying for something different"—to the bizarre—shaking the Dead President Malaise that seemed to hold the country in a death grip.

There is, however, no question about what the Beatles and their compatriots actually did. They repackaged American rhythm and blues and sold it back to the consumer who was most familiar with the original product, but now wouldn't touch it with a ten-foot pole—the trusty American teen.

Perhaps the phenomenal success of the British Invasion lies in that repackaging. The Beatles offered a way out of the racial dilemma that had gripped rock and roll since its beginnings, because they were neither white nor black—they were *English!* Given most Americans' shaky notions about the rest of the world, to be English with those cute little accents and natty Mod suits and all that hair was only slightly removed from being jolly green Martians.

For aliens, be they from Britain or Alpha Centauri, all

the rules were suspended. To Americans, these weren't white boys singing the blues, although that indeed was what they were, but *Englishmen* singing the blues. In the cold hard light of the 1980s such a distinction might seem childish in the extreme, but so do most negotiated settlements between warring nations. And while rock and roll might not have been a war, it was, as we have seen in Memphis, Tennessee, at the very least a total revolution in the way young people related to their world. The British Invasion allowed kids to sidestep the issue of race, of nigger music and white niggers, of who was stealing what from whom. For the first time *everybody* could embrace the new music without fear of having the color rub off. Pretty soon little girls were passing out from sheer ecstasy at Shea Stadium and Mom and Pop were once again shaking their heads sadly, wondering for the second time in just ten years how things had gotten this far out of hand, and where it would all end.

British music is a carnival funhouse mirror reflection of the American musical scene. This is not quite fair but more than a little true. In the beginning rock and roll was peculiarly American because only in America did the cultures of black and white have the chance to interact on a continuing basis. When the rock and roll explosion of the 1950s began in earnest, the rest of the world looked on in awe for a couple of minutes, then followed suit. Pretty soon there were Japanese Elvises and Mexican Elvises (country singer Freddy Fender, in fact, began his career in the mid-1950s as "the Mexican Elvis") and, of course, British Elvises. As Greg Shaw, editor of several rock magazines and authority on England's contribution to rock, has pointed out, the shared language alone was enough to guarantee the importation of rock and roll into England.

But here's where the funhouse mirror takes effect. In England the groups backing the singer became stars in their own right, whereas in America the singer was the focal point of the revolution and the band was strictly secondary. What were the Comets without Bill Haley? The Crickets without Buddy Holly? In fact, many rock-abilly singers in the South toured without any band at all (as many country singers still do), content to use whatever was available at the local bar. In England, however, thanks especially to Cliff Richard and the Shadows, the cult of the group was born.

The reasons for the explosion of British groups in the early 1960s can be traced directly to the late 1950s craze for "skiffle" music, an Anglicized version of American folk music that reached its height with the overwhelming successes of Lonnie Donegan, who even managed a hit on the American charts in 1961 with "Does Your Chewing Gum Lose Its Flavor on the Bedpost Overnight?" Apparently everyone in the entire country under the age of twenty formed a skiffle band and set out to make a local name for themselves. When *that* didn't work, they had to turn to something else, and to a large extent they turned to American black music.

The British fascination with American black music does indeed defy analysis, at least from this side of the Atlantic. What happened was that around 1961 all those kids with bands discovered that skiffle just didn't cut it in the British equivalents of honky-tonks. Folk music was okay in the living room, but it refused to translate to the sweaty working-class bars in such industrial enclaves as Liverpool. So they looked across the Atlantic and decided to cop the wild-man rock and roll and rhythm and blues for their own bar dates. "Obviously," wrote Greg Shaw in the liner notes for an album of English rock, "none of the English groups could hope to match the original mania of their idols, but they needed this sort of material to survive in the conditions under which they were performing, and it could even be conjectured that the strength of the material tended to bring out reservoirs of raunch that British teenagers had been led to believe they couldn't possess. So they threw themselves into the music with utter abandon, and if they couldn't be truly deranged, they could at least be energetic."

So the British groups began sifting through American black music with a vengeance, appropriating obscure Motown material from such black artists as Solomon Burke, Arthur Alexander, Sam Cooke, Joe Turner, and other underappreciated singers, not to mention such standards as Chuck Berry, Bo Diddley, Little Richard, and Fats Domino; rhythm and blues icons like Muddy Waters, Howlin' Wolf, and Big Bill Broonzy; and girl groups like the Shirelles, until it seemed like the Underground Railroad was operating once again, this time running escaped slave songs to England.

To be sure, the British groups also expropriated American rockabilly, but it was with the strictly black forms that the groups really found their groove. Predictably, along about 1962 there was a schism in British rock that neatly reflected the schism building in American black music. On the one side were the Mersey Beat people like the Beatles, Freddie and the Dreamers, the Dave Clark Five (more an American phenomenon than English), and the like, whose specialty was what came to be called "pop" music—recycled Motown, girl-group stuff, lightweight, good-time music. On the other was a group of malcontents in London, most notably the Rolling Stones, John Mayall, Brian Auger, and similar soul brothers, who were committed to "pure" blues, reflecting the American break between the Motown organization, with its "lightened" black music, and the old-time rhythm and blues performers, whose music was "too black" to be commercial.

Of all the blues "purists" in London in the early 1960s, John Mayall was perhaps the most "pure." Born in Manchester on November 29, 1933, Mayall grew up the son of a jazz musician in a house stocked with records of all sorts. By the age of thirteen he was enamored of the blues, but it wasn't until he was in college that he went to London to form the first of his many "Bluesbreakers" bands. Those bands have been called finishing schools for some of England's most influential pop instrumentalists, including Eric Clapton, the dean of British rock guitarists and one of the foremost proponents of the blues guitar; John McVie and Peter Green of the original Fleetwood Mac; Mick Taylor of the Rolling Stones; and Jack Bruce of Cream (with Clapton). Mayall has been described as a relentless taskmaster who insisted that his bands rehearse extensively and have a thorough knowledge of the music they were playing. He was also relentless about demanding recognition for the original American blues singers, waging at times what seemed to be a single-man crusade in the face of vast audience indifference.

After the first set, which featured a host of blues standards, each prefaced by Mayall's recitation of the original artist, I managed to strike exactly the wrong note backstage by mentioning the phrase "black music."

"What is *black* music?" Mayall snapped. "Music isn't black or white. There's no such thing as *black* music."

And, of course, he's absolutely right—now. The British Invasion was the death knell for black music in America because the music was ever so much more successful when performed by ersatz black Englishmen than by ratty old American blacks. (Lloyd Grossman, who is English, made the point in his *A Social History of Rock Music* that one might find, say, Chubby Checker pumping gas down the street in Anytown, U.S.A., while the Beatles would *never* sink to something so mundane.) But that's hardly what John Mayall meant.

"That's [the blues] what I grew up with. That's what I first heard," Mayall said. "It's always been a part of me. . . . It's all I ever heard—we didn't have a radio."

His father's jazz collection was extensive and wide-ranging, from Django Reinhardt to Louis Armstrong, and soon young John was working with his father's guitar. "I didn't start playing with the Bluesbreakers, with professional bands, until I was thirty. So you take the first thirty years of development, or nondevelopment, whatever you want to call it, that's thirty years of absorbing just about everything that was American black music . . ."

A contradiction . . .

". . . and in the course of that, American *white* music—jazz and blues and rock and roll, that's what I was brought up on."

The air in the dressing room remained chill as I kept rephrasing questions, trying to get at the fascination with American black music, music which John Mayall said didn't exist.

"Well, I don't know," he said. "It's my point of view. And probably what it will all come down to is that I was brought up on the music rather than the people—they could have been yellow or fucking pink or whatever color they wanted to be. The important thing is American culture, which is where it all comes from. You see, America is a unique country, and I think you'll find that if you talk to any other European, black, or white, or . . . go to Japan, you'll get yellows there, everybody has been brought up on American music. It's not just black music; it's American music."

I was reminded of a recent conversation with a music researcher, the beneficiary of numerous grants to study the phenomenon of American popular music. "Half of the problem in sorting out heads from tails these days is the goddammed British," he said ruefully. "They've sifted through American pop music with a fine-toothed comb, and their research is meticulous to the very extreme. Every time someone coughed at a Sun recording session in Memphis, it is recorded in English research. But despite all the research, I think the English have a sort of basic misunderstanding of what this music is all about. They know every detail of our musical history, and they publish reams of material about it, but somewhere right at the very beginning they missed a basic connection."

"I think," said John Mayall, "that people who lived and grew up outside the U.S. took a bigger interest in American music because they didn't have personal, direct access to it. So they learned more about it than any American."

The very best students were the Beatles, who changed the whole ballgame. They composed much of their own music; they were a group without an obvious front man; they sang in harmonies; they were clean—and the American response was staggering. Of course, there was a chorus of groans, of anti-Beatle, anti-rock sentiment from the older generation, but the protest was strangely without substance. All the vehemence was feigned, because the Beatles were infinitely preferable to a rejuvenated Elvis Presley or Chuck Berry. Even the scruffier, harder-edged, more working-class Rolling Stones were easier to take than the infinitely more threatening homegrown product.

The Beatles broke down the door for about a million other English groups (the Searchers, the Hollies, the Animals, Gerry and the Pacemakers, Billy J. Kramer and the Dakotas, Peter and Gordon, Them, the Kinks, the Who, the Bee Gees, Freddie and the Dreamers, Manfred Mann, the Silkie, Donovan, Wayne Fontana and the Mindbenders, and so on and so forth), including the miscreants in the London blues scene, most notably the Rolling Stones. The real breakthrough, though, came in 1966 when Eric Clapton and Jack Bruce left John Mayall to launch Cream (along with drummer Ginger Baker), the first of what we might call the "modern" rock groups.

By 1966 the British Invasion was beginning to fray around the cuffs, and the hits for that year swung wildly between Frank Sinatra's "Strangers in the Night" and Percy Sledge's "When a Man Loves a Woman," the first pop success by a black soul singer. In a brief period of two months the charts could go from Nancy Sinatra singing about boots to Sergeant Barry Sadler singing about the Green Berets to the Young Rascals (once described as the blackest-sounding white group to ever come out of the Northeast) singing about good lovin'. With the

Monkees and the Strawberry Alarm Clock on the horizon, disgruntled listeners began looking for something reliable to listen to, and fledgling FM radio was happy to oblige. Drawing from albums rather than singles and tapping into what would soon be called Flower Power or the Youth Movement or the Counterculture, FM radio played music different from that on AM, and one of the staples of "underground" FM was the British blues coterie led by Eric Clapton and Cream, the first "heavy-metal" rock group.

Originally Clapton saw the group as a "blues" trio, playing loud, long, electric blues à la Muddy Waters or B. B. King and, for all intents and purposes, remaining unknown except to blues aficionados. But Cream succeeded beyond anyone's wildest imagination—by the time of the *Disraeli Gears* album in 1967 Cream had captured the "underground" market.

The music that Clapton and crew played was indeed blues-based—he'd learned his lessons from John Mayall quite well, and he shared his mentor's love of things American. In particular, Clapton was fascinated by the short life of bluesman Robert Johnson. His recording of one of Johnson's songs, "Crossroads," with Cream turned that song into a virtual FM anthem. Cream played long, loud blues, with Clapton's guitar improvisations leading the way. Like the Beatles before them, Cream blasted down the doors for other British and American "blues" groups, including Clapton's mentor's Bluesbreakers and such American advocates of white blues ("blue-eyed soul," it was derogatorily called) as Paul Butterfield and his Blues Band.

As interesting as the music, perhaps, are the *semantics*. Cream and its clones billed themselves as "blues" groups, as much to differentiate themselves from the pop music of the times as to define the kind of music they were playing. Initially FM disk jockeys gave long explanations of how these were *white* groups doing the blues . . . actually extrapolations of the blues, extensions of the original licks pioneered by itinerant black singers in the South. Eventually, as might be predicted, the novelty wore thin. By 1969 *Rolling Stone* magazine, the undisputed voice of popular music and young America, could carry an ad for an unknown English singer named Joe Cocker that featured the memorable lines, "You can't cover your skin with chocolate syrup and call it bar-b-que." The ad goes on to point out, in the grand British Invasion style, that the blues aren't black or white, but human, and that Joe Cocker is the greatest (white) male blues singer alive today. Ummmmmmmm. . . .

The central question changed from Can a white man sing the blues? to Can a *black* man sing the blues? because after Cream the whites had the terminology all sewed up. With the skill of a surgeon, popular culture removed "black" from "blues" leaving the term free to become almost synonymous with British groups in the Mayall cast. It was the triumph of the British contention that music was without color and the American dis-ease of coming to terms with rock and roll.

Rock and roll was initially *more* than a white man singing the blues—it was a spark that arced between the two cultures, black and white. That spark had to be extinguished.

"Europe has always been renowned for having a real thirst for anything to do with American culture, whether it be novels, movies, and particularly music, which we grew up with, on the records, as long as records have been out," said John Mayall, warming to the subject. "People in Europe tend to know who's playing on what 78 [rpm record] that was made back in 1945. I mean, we know all that, 'cause that's all we have—the records. . . . We took it [the music] seriously and absorbed it deeply, and then it became us. . . . Blues is a universal language."

He's right about that, of course. No music is the exclusive province of any one group. But one is awed by the ease with which popular culture—practically by definition lily white—appropriated the elements of black culture. Not that white boys couldn't sing the blues, because, as we've seen in the earlier chapters, musical forms constantly shifted between black and white almost from the moment the first slave ship arrived in America. Not every musician shares Mayall's obsession with seeing that credit, and money, are given where due. And for every Eric Clapton, who personally arranged for bluesman Skip James to get not only credit but royalties, there's at least one Led Zeppelin to lift Willie Dixon's "You Need Love" and turn it into "Whole Lotta Love," an international smash hit, without so much as a tip of the hat to the original. More importantly, there is something I call the Steamroller Effect in operation.

Once the blues were cut loose from blacks, in no time at all blacks became slightly seamy, as if *they* were swiping the blues from the British groups. In short, in popular music as in popular culture, the stronger always steamroll over the weaker, until there is nothing left but a little flat smear on the concrete. To be sure, some blacks did profit from the British Invasion and British blues, most notably B. B. King, who after years of relative obscurity on Beale Street in Memphis parlayed success in England into commercial success in America, and James Brown, who correctly reasoned that given the success of imitation black music, there must be some kind of audience, however small, for the real thing. In the mid-1960s Brown assembled a band, a plethora of background singers, and hit the road as the ultimate expression of black music. Pretty soon he was pulling in the white audience by sheer flamboyance.

For the most part, though, the Steamroller Effect managed to keep black artists in their place while white imitation groups rolled up success after success. Even today, comparing the success of, say, Eric Clapton to that of B. B. King is like talking in different languages. While B. B. might be doing all right, Clapton is only slightly less than royalty. The two artists might as well be living in different universes.

The British notion of the universality of music has been accepted as gospel, and now it is usually used against blacks when they get uppity and start talking about *their* music. During one of the regular blues "revivals" in Memphis, the Home of the Blues, white groups who played the blues were welcomed with open arms, while black soul musicians, then one of Memphis' biggest industries—people who had learned the blues in a way no white kid from New Jersey could ever hope to and who were the true heirs to the blues tradition—were shunned. Music has no *color*, man. Don't come telling us about how black you are.

MOTOWN:
A CHOICE OF COLORS?

Motown itself called the Motown Sound "a stylized reflection of Afro-American tradition," and that's what it was: Afro-American tradition updated by the incessant pounding of the punch press and buffed to a shiny gloss by contact with a prosperous urban society.
—The Story of Motown,
by Peter Benjaminson

The only American record label to weather the British Invasion, indeed, actually thrive, was Motown, the sole black record company in America. This is ironic because while the British white boys were expropriating the blues, Motown had apparently struck a deal with the White Devil: Let us be successful, Boss, and we promise not to remind you too much that we're black.

In fact, in 1964 when the mania was just gearing up, Motown scored four No. 1 hits (one by Mary Wells, "My Guy," and three by the Supremes, "Where Did Our Love

Go," "Baby Love," and "Come See About Me") and a slew of not-so-popular hits that would eventually become rock and roll standards—"Dancing in the Streets" by Martha and the Vandellas, "Baby I Need Your Loving" by the Four Tops, "You're a Wonderful One" by Marvin Gaye, among them. The next year, while the top of the charts seemed to rotate between the Beatles, the Beach Boys, and the Supremes, Motown churned out such classics as "How Sweet It Is to Be Loved by You" (Marvin Gaye), "My Girl" (the Temptations), "Nowhere to Run" (Martha and the Vandellas), "Shotgun" (Junior Walker), "Ooo Baby Baby" (the Miracles), "I Can't Help Myself" (the Four Tops), "It's the Same Old Song" (the Four Tops), "The Tracks of My Tears" (the Miracles), and other lesser-known, much-rerecorded works.

The secret of the Motown Sound, the exact terms of the deal with the Devil, had two aspects. The first was neatly summed up by Motown recording artist, ace songwriter, and corporate vice-president Smokey Robinson (of Smokey Robinson and the Miracles) in a 1970 interview: "Don't get me wrong, now, this is a beautiful history period for black people," he said. "But there's a time and place for everything, I think. I'm proud of my blackness, sure, but I don't think the stage is a place to lecture about it. The people come to be entertained." The second part of the secret of the Motown Sound came from Africa, by way of the church. Every Motown song had the beat, and black or white, when you heard one of those songs, you wanted to *dance*.

When ex-featherweight boxer Berry Gordy, recent alumnus of Detroit's auto assembly lines, decided to launch his own record company in January 1959, he had an unswerving belief in two ideas: the assembly line was the most efficient way to manufacture anything, and the sole way to beat the odds was to produce only winners. Accordingly, his Motown Records, named for his hometown of Detroit and started with $800 in borrowed money, was set up as a musical assembly line whose end products were all designed to be hits. Had Gordy known more about the music business, perhaps he would have realized how ridiculous his ideas were—a *black* record company run by a *black* man whose avowed goal was to produce only *hit* records. And not just rhythm and blues hits, either, but *pop* hits.

Not that most record companies don't start out to make only hits. It's just that after about the fourth or fifth release the sheer reality of the numbers starts getting to them—there are hundreds of other companies, all staffed by men with glowing eyes and an unswerving belief that their records are the best records in the world, if only people would listen to them.

Berry Gordy seemed an unlikely hitmaker. Born in 1929 to a fairly well-to-do black family on the edge of Detroit's teeming ghetto, Gordy drifted into boxing almost as an excuse to keep away from his parents' businesses, including a print shop he despised. He was an unpredictable fighter, and he drifted out of the ring just in time for the Korean War in 1951. After the war he parlayed his love of jazz and every cent he could beg or borrow into a record store, just in time to get clobbered by rock and roll. The first rock explosion of the mid-1950s left little standing in its wake, and in 1955 Gordy's jazz-oriented record store sank like a stone. In Detroit, when you've finally run out of options, there's always the factories, which is where Gordy headed. For the next two years, until 1957, he spent his days sticking chrome trim on Lincolns and Mercurys, adjusting the music running through his head to the steady beat of the factory. After a while he realized that the music in his head was not a repeat of last night's radio broadcasts, it was something new and original, and he began to write it down in the evenings after work.

In July of 1957 Gordy was so sure of that music that he quit the assembly line to become a full-time songwriter. He envisioned himself supplying all the local talent in Detroit with songs, but it wasn't until he ran into an old friend from his fight days, Jackie Wilson, that things really began happening. He wrote four songs for Wilson, a fledgling singer. The fourth was "Lonely Teardrops," a monster hit that established Wilson's reputation as a vocalist. The other three were also hits, and Gordy was instantly established as a major songwriter.

Ever the drifter, Gordy refused to be satisfied with any one thing. According to Motown biographer Peter Benjaminson, the collapse of the record store years before had left Gordy with a virtually insatiable craving for success in every area. Also, and ultimately more importantly, the music Gordy heard in his head was not always the music that came off the records of his songs. Too many other people had a hand in the recording process, and in Gordy's view the product was hopelessly diluted by the time it got to the radio.

So Gordy turned to production, leasing the final product to major companies for release. Finally he launched Motown in January 1959.

Motown's first employee was Alan Abrams, who was white. Stax Records, which would grow to be Motown's major rival in black music in the 1960s, was being launched in Memphis, Tennessee, around the same time by Jim Stewart and his sister, Estelle Axton, both white. The second employee they hired—David Porter—was black.

Gordy already knew what numerous other independent record entrepreneurs were discovering: Once the rabbit warrens of New York and Los Angeles were left behind, nobody much gave a damn about local talent. Sun Records in Memphis, King Records in Cincinnati, Chess Records in Chicago, and dozens of others began their businesses by exploiting the local talent overlooked by the established, petrified companies. The huge record conglomerates at times resemble the legendary farmer's jackass, whose attention span is roughly equal to the length of the two-by-four plank you hit him with. With the rock and roll fever apparently under control, major companies like CBS and RCA were content to sit back smugly and control the business from their East and West Coast bunkers until some trend, like the Twist from Philadelphia, smacked them in the face.

So Gordy turned to the turf he knew best, the Detroit ghetto, and started plucking out gems, the first of which was the Miracles, featuring Smokey Robinson. He followed them with the Temptations, formed in 1961 and launched into rock and roll history in 1965 with "My Girl," written by Smokey Robinson; Martha Reeves and the Vandellas, good for such classics as "Heat Wave," "Dancing in the Streets," and "Jimmy Mack"; the Marvelettes, of "Please Mr. Postman" fame; and many others.

By 1961 Gordy had the groove, the Motown Sound. That year brought the Miracles their first success, "Shop Around," as well as the Marvelettes' "Please Mr. Postman." The next year saw six Motown songs on the charts. Like a factory foreman getting the bugs worked out of his assembly line, Gordy tinkered with the Motown Sound until it sounded just like the music in his head.

A couple of things were readily apparent to Gordy: real success meant capturing the white market, and capturing the white market meant not coming on *too* black. Rhythm, Gordy said—the black beat—is what people wanted; the trick was to disguise the black roots. After all, the beat had always been present in black music, but until that beat was made palatable for whites, as it had been by Elvis Presley and the other rockers, whites wouldn't touch it.

So Gordy followed his nose for money and looked at the most lucrative performers' circuit in the country, the Vegas nightclubs, to see what the monied class were listening to. He heard strings and orchestral arrangements—in a word, class. The rich folks wanted happy music, sophisticated upbeat stuff that would leave them smiling.

Motown's forays into social commentary, such as the Temptations' "Ball of Confusion" in 1970 or the Supremes' "Love Child" in 1968 (written by Canadian R. Dean Taylor, Motown's only white songwriter), didn't sound any more authentic than their forays into psychedelia à *la* the Temptations' "Psychedelic Shack" in 1970.

So that's what Motown would become—a gospel beat with a touch of class, just like Vegas. "Motown music was almost always upbeat," wrote Mike Freedberg in an analysis of 1960 black music, "because a beat had more universal appeal than soul ballads, and Motown's upbeat was a metallic thing that spoke to anyone who lived in the world of machine noise." The sheer energy of the music was enough to get you on your feet, and the beat would get you moving (*Rolling Stone* commented that you *felt* a Motown song in your guts before your ears actually heard it).

But Gordy was always careful to add enough "class" to make the music acceptable to whites. His arrangements were lush, a gooey featherbed of strings and orchestration that tried its best to belie the beat. The touch of class extended to the acts themselves. Consider, say, the Supremes' album covers from the early days of the mid-1960s—little Kewpie dolls in outrageous dresses and fixed smiles and light complexions, sort of mock-Negroes in spike heels and wigs. When the first burst of black consciousness hit in the late 1960s, the Supremes got hundreds of letters from sincere fans urging them to let their tortured hair relax in a natural Afro. No dice—the wigs stayed.

Motown had a sort of finishing school for its largely unpolished artists. The school began with the very basics of style, from which fork to use for the salad to diction to personal hygiene. From there, the school went on to stage manners, costumes, and choreography—in fact, Motown acts became legendary for their slick stage shows, so that cartoonist Garry Trudeau could make the coordinated moves of Gladys Knight and the Pips a running joke throughout the mid-1970s in his *Doonesbury* comic strip.

Attendance at school was mandatory, but the Motown acts seldom resisted. Part of the Motown plan was to place artists in the swank Vegas supper clubs and the largely white world of television, and since Gordy had delivered on everything else, there was no reason to think he wouldn't deliver on this. Go to class to get class.

And deliver Gordy did. The list of Motown's successes is almost scary: the Supremes (with Diana Ross), the Temptations, the Four Tops, the Jackson Five, Stevie Wonder, Marvin Gaye, Gladys Knight and the Pips, Smokey Robinson and the Miracles, the Spinners, the Marvelettes, Martha Reeves and the Vandellas, Mary Wells, the Isley Brothers, Junior Walker and the All-Stars, Tammi Terrell, all conspired to make an indelible imprint on the 1960s and 1970s.

The real achievement, however, was that Motown became such a force that it *was* black music in the 1960s. The white boys had already staked out the blues as their territory. Now Motown's upbeat white-ified rhythm and blues overshadowed the soul men of Stax Records with their unabashed gospel deliveries in front of the chunky, wailing southern bar music that was a Stax trademark.

"I think there is a great void in black music today—a great void," fretted Phil Spector in 1969. Spector, the producer of such groups as the Ronettes ("Walking in the Rain"), the Teddy Bears ("To Know Him Is to Love Him"), and the Crystals ("He's a Rebel"), staked out his territory as one of rock's most innovative and talented producers. "What has disappeared completely is the black groups, other than what you have coming out of Motown and a few others—and I don't mean Stax-Volt, because I don't consider that what I'm talking about. The group on the corner has disappeared. It's turned into a white psychedelic group or a guitar group, there are thousands of them. There used to be hundreds and hundreds of black groups singing harmony and with a great lead singer and you'd go in and record them. You used to go down to Jefferson High or 49th and Broadway and could get sixteen groups. Today you can't find them.

"I mean, Motown has got it all tied up," he continued in that *Rolling Stone* interview, one of the few interviews he ever gave. "Stax doesn't even come near Motown. They can't get a special on television or anything. So who's dominating it? . . . I don't consider Motown black; I consider them half and half. Black people making white music."

Imagine two poles of power—Motown and Stax. Ironically, Motown was white music produced by blacks, while Stax was black music produced by whites. The Stax soul men—Otis Redding, Wilson Pickett, Eddie Floyd, Sam and Dave, Johnny Taylor, to name a few—were everything Motown's R & B cadets weren't. They were soulful, visceral, sensual, sexy, and, above all, they were *black*. No matter that their record company and most of their backup musicians were white—Memphis, the home of Stax, had a long history of mixing the musical colors. But nothing could stand against you-can-dance-to-it Motown Sound.

By 1970 it was obvious that Motown had painted itself into a very lucrative corner; it was time for the beat to move on. And move it did, right about the time Motown decided to move itself out of Motor City to the gold-paved highways of Los Angeles, to make yet another fortune in the movie business. The beat drifted on to Philadelphia, into the hands of producers Thom Bell, Kenny Gamble, and Leon Huff, who realized on some kind of gut level that they had to out-Motown Motown. It was a new decade and it was time to get on another train.

In short, it was time to party. Philly rhythm and blues took up the Motown formula with a vengeance, adding even more strings and "sweetening." Motown refugees such as the Spinners found the groove with Thom Bell and such hits as "One of a Kind" and "Could It Be I'm Falling in Love"; the O'Jays, from the Gamble and Huff stable, recorded "Love Train" and "For the Love of Money." The Philly Sound was real: rhythm and blues with *class*—and you could dance to it.

THE SOLID
SOUL-TIDE REVUE

To an even greater extent than with country rock (rockabilly), the Memphis soul sound was the product of black and white people working together.

> —Charlie Gillett, writing in
> *The Sound of the City*

Memphis is just a big ole overgrown country town. That's all we are.

> —Estelle Axton, co-founder
> of Stax Records

There is a tendency to think of the soul music explosion in Memphis in the 1960s as something entirely separate from Sun Records, which is seen as entirely separate from the blues. In truth, the three form a single musical continuum, fueled by the continuous grinding of black against white. Musicians moved freely from one wave to the next, as exemplified by Rufus Thomas. Thomas be-

gan his career in the mid-1930s, touring with the legendary Rabbit Foot Minstrels as a song-and-dance man and
comic. From there he moved to WDIA as a disc jockey,
performing now and then in the clubs along Beale Street.
He recorded one of the first hits for Sam Phillips' fledgling Sun label ("Bear Cat," in 1953), and turned the
same trick for the newly formed Stax Records almost ten
years later with "The Dog" (1962) and "Walkin' the
Dog" (1963). He also claims to have recorded some of the
last hits for Stax, while the company was going down in
flames—but we are getting ahead of ourselves.

With the rockabilly fury ebbing rapidly (ironically, because of the total national acceptance of rock and roll),
the next wave in the Memphis boiling pot was already
building. That wave was laughingly referred to by James
Luther Dickinson as "suburban rock," both a reaction
and a response to Sun Records and the blues.

With Beale Street clearly in decline, its music was
forced out to the reaches of the sprawling city. Sunbeam
Mitchell, the famous impresario of Club Handy, had
opened a second club, Club Paradise (first show: Count
Basie, Bobby "Blue" Bland, and Howlin' Wolf) on the
outskirts of town. The music also found its way across the
Mississippi River to West Memphis, Arkansas, which was
the kind of city even its mother couldn't love, consisting
as it did of a dog track, a Mexican restaurant, and a
seemingly unlimited number of honky-tonks. One of
those 'tonks was called the Plantation Inn, and the entertainment consisted primarily of brawls, knife fights, and
music, usually in that order. The Plantation Inn drew
white kids from Memphis like molasses drew flies. The
city's suburbs were taking on a deadening sameness (in
my suburb the only honky-tonk for miles around was

bulldozed and replaced by a Methodist Church), and by the beginning of the 1960s, the city had already begun its search-and-destroy missions into the countryside around Beale Street. Anyway, rock and roll wasn't Beale Street's style. In the 1950s the focus had shifted from Beale to 706 Union. Now it was getting ready to shift again, and the Plantation Inn looked like as good a place as any.

Some of the kids who frequented the Plantation Inn were doing more than hanging out with blacks. They were soaking up the sound they heard, and pretty soon they arrived at a conclusion that probably ought to be carved in granite over the entrance to City Hall in Memphis: "Hell," the white boys thought, "I can do *that!*"

"I mean, hanging out with niggers was *fun,*" says Jim Dickinson. "That's why we all did it."

The music was a weird brew that could only come from Memphis. It drew on everything from jump blues to big-band music, rockabilly to jazz. What characterized it best was an easy, flowing rhythm, an infectious beat led by maybe an organ and a saxophone, with a guitar lead alongside for good measure. It was music you could dance to, music that made your body twitch, but it went way, way beyond dance music. It retained that rockabilly sense of clenched teeth, much like the honky-tonks themselves, where everybody could be dancing along having a great time one minute and carving up one another with broken bottles the next.

One of the bands that hung around the Plantation was called the Mar-Keys, a group from the lily-white confines of Messick High School. The band originally consisted of Duck Dunn, Steve Cropper, Don Nix, Charlie Freeman, and Packy Axton, and what set them apart from dozens of other white boys was that Packy Axton's mother, Estelle, owned a recording studio with her brother, Jim Stewart. Originally, Jim Stewart was a country fiddle player, but he went to college and got turned on, as they say, to classical music. He changed his fiddle for a violin and left school with an overwhelming urge to record music. ("It's a disease," Jim Dickinson says. "Once you catch it, you're done.")

Stewart's earlier studios in the back of a grocery store and a garage didn't satisfy—"We wanted to be where the talent was," Estelle Axton says—so they rented a bankrupt theater, the Capitol, on McClemore Street for $100 a month and founded the Satellite Studio. Using lots of volunteer labor, Stewart and Axton split the theater in half, making part of the stage a control room. Both of them kept their day jobs. "Money," Estelle Axton says, "wasn't too plentiful. We were doing the studio on the side, and we needed money to live on." Estelle insisted on opening a record store in the front of the theater because she was absolutely convinced that if she could see what people were buying, she and Stewart would know what to record. She was right.

Packy Axton led the Mar-Keys to his mother's studios, and the group began trying to put the Plantation honky-tonk feel on tape. Charlie Freeman drifted off, others drifted in, and eventually the group got it—in a single called "Last Night." That song was a hit, and some label in California starting bitching that they owned the rights to the Satellite name. So Stewart and Axton put their heads together and came up with Stax: ST for Stewart; AX for Axton.

In 1961 Stax was a going concern, and the Mar-Keys hit the road to promote "Last Night." They played the sleaziest, blackest honky-tonks in the country, places where, as Ronnie Hawkins would later say, you had to puke twice and show your razor before they'd let you in. With the Mar-Keys went sixteen-year-old Carla Thomas, who'd had Stax's second hit, "Gee Whiz," chaperoned by Estelle Axton. Actually, "Gee Whiz" was cut for Atco, the pop label for Atlantic, which had begun distributing Stax. "Atlantic gave us a thousand dollars, and that was the biggest thousand dollars I've ever seen in my life," Estelle Axton says. Estelle and Carla lasted for about half the tour—"The boys," Estelle says with affection, "were such cut-ups." Not even Elvis, commented Memphis writer Stanley Booth years later, got away with what the Mar-Keys got away with. It was similar to snow-white Buddy Holly playing the coal-black Apollo in New York City a few years before—nobody told him he *wasn't* supposed to play there. Nobody told the Mar-Keys that they *couldn't* play the chitlin' circuit, so they did.

The Mar-Keys might have gone down as just another bunch of high school rockers if Stax Records hadn't been in the right place at the right time. Talent was literally walking in off the street, and Stewart and Axton knew how to take advantage of it. Cropper and Dunn left the Mar-Keys to join two blacks—Booker T. Jones, an organ player, and Al Jackson, Jr., the son of a legendary Memphis music figure around Beale Street and a pretty fair drummer himself—to form Booker T. and the M.G.'s. The M.G.'s had a hit in 1962 with the instrumental "Green Onions," and they became the house band at Stax, backing anyone who came into the studio. Their music was "suburban rock," a cleaned-up, *whitened* version of what they had heard at the Plantation Inn. One of the most important people to walk in off the street was a gospel-style singer from Macon, Georgia, named Otis Redding.

Not to say that Otis was the first gospel-style black singer. Actually, the style was a venerable staple in black music, and such singers as Ray Charles and Sam Cooke had made strong inroads into the white market with their "churchy" sound. But they paid a price for success. Their arrangements were soft, emulating the crooner style of Perry Como or even Pat Boone. In fact, the arranger was one of the most important persons at recording sessions for most black artists, if not *the* most important. Recording was done by the numbers: the arranger wrote a score and the musicians dutifully followed it.

But Memphis had always been a haphazard place where the musicians put their own arrangements together as they went along, and Stax was no exception. There are at least a dozen different versions of Otis Redding's arrival at Stax. He'd been working with moderate success (meaning he wasn't starving) when, at the insistence of his white manager and close friend Phil Walden (who went on to found and lose Capicorn Records, the home of the Allman Brothers Band), he came to Memphis with another local Macon group, the Pinetoppers, to audition for Stewart. According to the best rags-to-riches version of the story, Otis drove the bus for the Pinetoppers, and just before the leader of the group, Johnny Jerkins, left the studio, he personally appealed to Stewart to listen to his bus driver sing . . . and the rest is history. Actually, Otis was scheduled to sing at that audition, where he cut "These Arms of Mine" and "Hey Hey Hey." Stewart didn't like the cuts—according to the people who worked for Stax, Stewart *never* liked Otis' music)—but the boys in the band heard something, and Otis was signed up.

With Otis, and later with Wilson Pickett (on Atlantic),

Sam and Dave, William Bell, Don Covey, and Eddie Floyd, Stax found its groove—the blending of punchy suburban rock with a gospel front man to make . . . soul music.

By 1964 Stax had soul all tied up, but there was one little catch. By 1964 the Beatles, playing refried rhythm and blues, had completely changed the ballgame. That year there were some 41-million-selling English singles and albums, by the Beatles, the Kinks, the Rolling Stones, the Dave Clark Five, and many others cashing in on the mania for anything with a British accent. Of the twenty-seven No. 1 songs throughout the next year, thirteen were by English groups. Right behind the British Invasion the West Coast was gearing up for the Endless Summer, with the Beach Boys, Jan and Dean, and the other surf-and-car groups. The only black artists to stand their ground in this onslaught were Berry Gordy's Motown groups. For the soul men in Memphis, the door was closed.

The door flew open, however, when all that shiny British chrome got a little tarnished. The first No. 1 soul song appeared in 1967, but it came not from Memphis but from Muscle Shoals—Percy Sledge's "When a Man Loves a Woman." Once again, the pure, unadulterated Memphis product was too strong, too harsh, too *real* to make it in the world of popular music. Take, for instance, the always shaky relationship between Atlantic Records in New York City and Stax. Atlantic began distributing Stax in 1960, and some of Atlantic's biggest black acts came to Memphis to record. Atlantic, with Jerry Wexler at the helm, prided itself on its handling of black artists— like the southern labels, it had gotten its start as a jazz and R & B outfit. But Wexler was always tense in

Memphis, never quite as comfortable as he thought he should be. And, conversely, Memphis was never altogether comfortable with someone from "outside," however talented he might be. (Memphis is still touchy about outsiders and "carpetbaggers." While talking to one oldtime Memphis musician, I happened to mention Walter Dawson, the longtime music critic for the *Commercial Appeal* and one of the most knowledgeable people about Memphis music. "Yeah," the old-timer said, "Walter's not a bad guy for an outsider." Walter came to Memphis in 1965.)

The best-known Wexler-Stax collaboration is Wilson Pickett's "Wait 'til the Midnight Hour," for which Wexler suggested a more danceable beat. "You got to remember," said Jim Dickinson, "that most of these guys at Stax didn't necessarily think what they were doing was any good. Memphis was always like that—it takes somebody from the outside to validate what we're doing."

A story is told (with relish) about one of Wexler's early trips to Memphis. He put up at the swank Hotel Peabody, famous for its ducks in the lobby. Wexler was nervous as a cat in a roomful of rocking chairs—there was a level of craziness in Memphis that defied New York analysis. The perfectly logical New York idea of a "liberal"—a white man who likes black men, who harbors no ill feelings because of race—hardly seemed to have meaning in a city where rednecks played nigger music. It was also a city of intense racial hatred, so Wexler's meeting with Rufus and Carla Thomas had to be on the sly. But when Rufus and Carla came up the back way to Wexler's room, the house dick spotted them. What he saw was a middle-aged black man leading a strikingly pretty young black girl upstairs to a white man's room. When the dick knocked on the door to find out what was happening, Wexler panicked. Clutching a letter he'd written to the New York office that explained where he was and what might happen to him, he shoved past the dick, raced down the steps to the street, and ran until he found the nearest mailbox. He stuffed the letter in, hoping that when it arrived in New York, the execution wouldn't have taken place just yet.

Even as Otis Redding was taking soul music to the masses at the Monterey Pop Festival in 1967 (the same festival that turned Janis Joplin into a superstar), the Memphis Sound was already wearing around the edges. It is the nature of music to change, perhaps more so in Memphis than elsewhere, simply because there is more music there. In Memphis music always seems chafing at the bit to evolve in a totally unself-conscious way. A producer, say, Chips Moman, gets tired of working for Stax and strikes out on his own. The results are the Boxtops and the Gentrys, in the first case the blackest-sounding white boys yet, in the second the group that produced one of the most danceable sounds of the 1960s. In the late 1960s veteran Stax producer Isaac Hayes returned to his first love, singing, and produced an album called *Hot Buttered Soul*, which had less to do with the Memphis Sound as defined by Stax than with Hayes' own gut feeling that people were getting ready to dance once again. By the end of 1970 *Hot Buttered Soul* was a platinum album. The next year Hayes provided the soundtrack for a movie about a black private eye named John Shaft, and the song "Shaft" was the biggest-selling and most influential record to come out of Memphis since the days of Elvis.

While Isaac Hayes was laying the groundwork for

disco and the slick Philadelphia Sound, across town
Willie Mitchell was busy turning another gospel singer
named Al Green into a superstar. In fact, it was the
"new" Memphis music—the dance music of Isaac Hayes
and the sexy ballads of Al Green—that launched the
1970s in high gear.

But it never seems to last. Trends begin in Memphis,
only to move on to bigger and better things. Sam Phillips
sells Elvis' contract for $35,000 and $5,000 in back royalties, and Sun Records becomes the only label that *no*
artist ever renewed a contract with. Stax Records, after
becoming the most influential studio in the 1960s, goes
down in flames, the victim of critical (at times criminal)
financial mismanagement. Al Jackson is killed "by a bur-
glar," and there are persistent rumors linking the murder
to Stax. Isaac Hayes begins believing his own press, and
drops as quickly as he rose. Al Green returns to the
church. Estelle Axton records a novelty hit called "Disco
Duck" and wonders what went wrong. Jim Stewart refuses to speak with reporters. About half the people who
recorded for Sun return to the church. Elvis dies. Producer Chips Moman moves to Nashville and begins producing Waylon Jennings. Producer Jack Clement from
Sun moves to Nashville and does eight gold records with
Charlie Pride. Producer Allen Reynolds from Sun moves
to Nashville and establishes Crystal Gayle as the hottest-
selling item since sliced bread. Behind them all are the
shuttered and staring eyes of Beale Street, the faintest
whisperings of the blues.

WHITE BLUES

Part of being a bluesman is a state of mind, an attitude, even a philosophy. . . . We had a lot to learn from the black people.
　　　　　　　　　　　　　　　　　　　　　　—Nick Gravenites

Being an urban Jewish boy, somehow I could relate easier to urban blacks than I could to Southern people.
　　　　　　　　　　　　　　　　　　　　—Michael Bloomfield

The British weren't alone in their fascination with American black music. In the late 1950s, at the very time British music was beginning to gear up and Berry Gordy was starting Motown, some American musicians were beginning to scratch the nearly impenetrable shell of the black community. Unlike the groundswell across the ocean, where every kid had a guitar and could name the five biggest-selling American black artists for each year since creation, the American white blues "movement" consisted of a very few people, mostly university students with an interest in "folk" music.

Unlike their British counterparts, the American white blues pioneers, especially in Chicago, had direct access to the authentic product on its home turf, the sleazy black clubs and honky-tonks. For them, the blues were more than an academic exercise; they were grimy rib joints and sweaty clubs where white people were only slightly less rare than talking bears, and the sheer novelty of a shiny-white university student was enough to keep him alive and tolerated.

The white blues kids were the last piece of the puzzle, the last brick to be mortared into place in the monolithic wall of modern rock and roll. These kids went one step beyond the British "blues" players; they were the fore-runners of the White Negro, that media creation of the late 1960s who set the tone for music in the 1970s. What they wanted, and what they got eventually, was accep-tance in the black community, an acknowledgment from *blacks* that a white boy could play the blues with the best of them.

These white blues kids got their acceptance in a way that has proved to be totally unique: they learned the music from the bottom up. They won acceptance in the black community because, and solely because, they were so damn *good*.

The white blues kids represent one of the last honest interchanges between black and white musicians. The very success of rock, which by the mid-1960s was success-ful beyond its wildest imagination, was already limiting the free flow of musical ideas. The civil rights movement unwittingly fueled the rush to the White Negro, which made any real involvement by whites in black culture harder and harder. The success of the music, coupled with the audience's growing urge to be something other than middle-class white kids, was a powerful draft for the industry, which realized immediately that not everybody in the world had John Mayall's intelligent sincerity or the white blues kids' almost savage intensity. In short, it was easier to create imitators.

Although the American white blues movement had outposts, it was centered in Chicago. There are several reasons for that, most of them bad. When the blues left Memphis, they took up permanent residence in the teeming South Side ghettoes of Chicago whose huge black population were mostly displaced southerners. There the blues completed the transformation from rural cry of pain into urban wail. The blues grew harder, more electric, and the beat began to pound in hundreds of clapboard bars and crumbling honky-tonks. Greats like Howlin' Wolf, Muddy Waters, Otis Rush, Willie Dixon, Otis Spann, and Sonny Boy Williamson, not to mention such pretenders to the throne as James Brown, Chuck Berry, and Bo Diddley, regularly played the clubs. Out-of-town talent routinely made the pilgrimage from the South to the South Side.

Like Beale Street in Memphis, the ghettoes of Chicago might as well have been on another planet. Whites were all but unknown there, and one could bet that whenever a white man showed up, it spelled trouble for somebody. In the middle of this black sea lies the University of Chicago, surrounded on three sides by ghetto and on one side by Lake Michigan. It was inevitable that the alien landscape around the university would exert a fatal attraction for some students, and indeed it did.

In 1960 the ghetto was a hostile place, teeming with real and imagined dangers, and the bulk of the university community was content to let it alone and go to frat parties, make good grades, and worry about creeping socialism and/or fascism. But the university did have an active folk music society, and that society defined folk music to include some of the less earthy blues. It didn't take long for a few members of the folk music society to realize that the music they were so intently listening to on record, the music of Big Bill Broonzy, Leadbelly, and Josh White, was also the music of the alien landscape around them.

"The music was all around us," remembers Norman Dayron, who, with Paul Butterfield, Nick Gravenites, and Elvin Bishop, formed the nucleus of the University of Chicago branch of the white blues kids. "There was just no way to avoid it. On a spring day people would be sitting out on their porches playing Charley Patton or Otis Rush. You just heard it everywhere."

So with fear and trepidation the white blues kids stepped over the line between the university and the ghetto, only to find somebody there ahead of them. His name was Michael Bloomfield, and his daddy was rich. More than anything else in the world, though, Michael Bloomfield wanted to become a bluesman.

"When I was around thirteen years old, I got into the radio," he says. "There were seven or eight black stations in Chicago, and two or three of those were aimed at the 'southern' market—they were stoned blues stations.

"Up until I was fifteen years old or so, I couldn't tell why I loved blues so much. I knew I loved rockabilly and the blues, and I couldn't hardly tell them apart. With a little more listening, I realized that all the guys I was enjoying on the radio and whose records and stuff I was buying were *playing* in clubs in Chicago."

So in 1959 Michael Bloomfield, well known as a hot-shot rock-and-roll guitar player in the swank Chicago suburbs, began hanging out in the black clubs of the South Side, filled with the all-consuming desire to play the blues. By the next year the sixteen-year-old white kid was sitting in, because he was very, very good.

So was Paul Butterfield, the university student who wanted to be a blues harmonica player. "The people who broke the color barrier were Bloomfield and Butterfield," says Nick Gravenites, no slouch at blockbusting himself. "They were the guys who could cut it musically. I re-member there was this place called the Blue Flame Lounge, and Butterfield would be the only white guy there. He was part of an all-black R & B review. At first he was a novelty act—white guy playing blues harmon-ica. But he'd knock them out. He was better than any of the people playing there, no matter *who* they were. And they *loved* this guy! He had a regular job there, and the first thing he'd do was go over to the shuffleboard game and beat them out of their money. Butterfield was an easygoing, big-hearted sort of guy. We called him 'Bunky.' "

If this sounds vaguely familiar—couple of white guys on the South Side of Chicago, one playing the harp, the other the guitar, both wanting to grow up to be blues-men—it's because you've seen it on *Saturday Night Live,* heard the multimillion-selling album, and by now seen the movie. Mike Bloomfield and Paul Butterfield were the models for the John Belushi–Dan Ackroyd creation, the Blues Brothers, the latest (and perhaps most famous) incarnation of white men singing the blues. (Of course, unlike Bloomfield and Butterfield, Belushi and Ackroyd are not very good, but they have made millions of bucks by pretending to be Negroes. This was once called minstrelsy, and the performers used to be in blackface.)

"I started going to those clubs beause I was nuts. Quote *nuts* unquote," says Gravenites, who after twenty years in the music business as a player and a producer still looks back fondly on the days in Chicago. "It took a certain amount of craziness to do it, and at that time in my life I was crazy. I was a hoodlum—used to carry a gun, that sort of thing. . . . I didn't care. I figured I would shoot somebody on one of those trips.

"See," he continues, "it was kind of a strange situation. I knew nothing about black people. My first introduction to black society was at the university. Otherwise I knew nothing, absolutely *nothing*. So I went in with this certain attitude. Well, the black had a different attitude altogether."

The clubs would periodically erupt in giant fights with guns, fists, knives, and bricks. There would be shouting, shooting, sirens, holes in the ceiling, busted bottles, but miraculously, no one would get hurt—at least not very badly.

"But the blacks knew that Whitey was crazy. Whitey couldn't take that kind of upfront shouting and screaming," Gravenites says. "Whitey'll pull a gun and kill ya." And, he adds, the blacks were well aware of what would happen if the morning's headlines read, "White Student Killed in Bar Brawl." Somebody black would do time, hard time. "Once you got used to what was happening, you realized that we were a whole lot more dangerous to them than they were to us. We'd pull the trigger. Felt real cocky and *white*, you know."

Sure, there was an element of danger, echoes Norman Dayron. "We were all a little more foolhardy, more willing to carry a gun. Nick was the first guy to pack a pistol, then some of the rest of us got guns—not that we ever used them. But we would have."

Dayron came to the University of Chicago from New York on a fellowship. But the fellowship didn't pay all the bills, so he needed a job for spending money. He ended up at Chess Records, the bastion of Chicago's black music scene. Norman Dayron, Ph.D. candidate, became the janitor. "I think they liked the idea of this university boy cleaning up after old black guys," he says ruefully. But his job at Chess threw him into the sphere of the white blues kids, and the fact that the black musicians recognized Dayron probably kept Gravenites from having to go for his piece on more than one occasion.

Granted, all this armament has an air of the dramatic, something Dayron at least is willing to admit: "There is the romance in being part of a culture that is totally alien to you." But is it so farfetched? I recall a few concerts I attended in Memphis, my home, with more than my wallet stuffed in my pocket, and I recall a few times when getting out was touch and go. Go ahead and wince, but remember that it is easier for a camel to pass through the eye of a needle than for a card-carrying liberal to pass into a black boogie club.

"I remember going to clubs where they'd never even *seen* white people except in newspapers, and even then they thought they were a shade of gray," says Norman Dayron. "I remember going to clubs where we were shot at with shotguns, where the clubs were blasted because we were white people and it ticked off racial relations."

The sole exception to all this melodrama was Bloomfield, the loner, who for a long time refused to become involved with the other white blues kids.

"Michael was totally naïve," says Dayron. "You know how it is when you're young—you don't believe anything can hurt you. Michael had that worse than anybody else. I was hip enough to be paranoid, to look around and see who was following me. Michael never did that. He was like an angel—good was protecting him. Water rolled off his back."

"I got beat up a lot," says Michael Bloomfield, not really laughing. "I got my ass whipped." But he gives the impression that the clobbering was a small price to pay, for he was obsessed with the blues, with being a part of the blues world. "At first, I wanted to be a greaser or something, an Elvis type of guy. But when I got into the blues scene, it was even more that way . . . I can't even find the words to describe what it was. If the Elvis-type guy was a wild and crazy guy, you know, then the blues guys were even cooler. They were the epitome of what I'd like to be, that sort of attitude. I loved it. That was exactly what I wanted to be and when I found myself being accepted by musicians who were older than me, accepting me as a peer, I really loved it."

Bloomfield sought out the aging blues musicians with a musicologist's passion. Eventually he operated a club where he could book the musicians, and for as long as they were there and getting paid, he would get them to teach him everything they knew. With Big Joe Williams, a bluesman who took the young white boy under his substantial wing, Bloomfield toured the South, searching the cotton fields and plain-dirt farms for every scrap of blues he could dig up. It was as if he'd apprenticed himself to the whole of the blues, and his greatest fear was that there wasn't enough of him to go around. "It made me feel as if I was being adopted into a big family, not only willing to give me affection and love, but also that I could have a Socratic relationship with them, as my teachers."

Perhaps the depth of Bloomfield's commitment can be measured by his answer to the question of what was so cool about the blues for a Jewish kid from the Chicago suburbs.

"Well, I guess it was strong," he says hesitantly. "It was intense, and their music had a sincerity to it . . . I'm not just talking about the blues *feeling* or anything . . . any mythological blues thing. It was just so strong and so vital and so powerful. That's what attracted me. You could stand up there and have this sort of power. . . . See, the whole music thing that I noticed, I picked it up more physically than intellectually. It was all sort of this call-and-response thing.

"When you played something, it was a lexicon, it was a language you had to learn. And when you could play in that language, the feedback you got then was of a very subtle nature. If you played the right note at the right time, there was a whole world of nuance that was understood. Just one note would bring back actual audible aural . . . someone would yell at you, *'Play it!'* or *'Get down!'* or whatever they would say at that time. There was a whole pattern of call and response . . . this sort of immediate feedback. It was different than people just applauding. They didn't applaud; they could follow you note by note and know exactly when you were playing right from the heart, and they'd give that heart right back to you. It was a language—the interplay."

So Africa came to Chicago, and popular music got

ready for another shot of the blues. Until then, Bloomfield had made a name for himself playing rock: "It was playing for people dancing, and they'd applaud when you were done playing. But this world of nuance didn't exist. Once I understood this world of nuance and I was getting feedback, it was a very enthralling and enrapturing feeling."

"Michael was so well known that he could just ascend the bandstand," says Norman Dayron. "He didn't have to ask to sit in anymore. That was a very high honor—he had an open invitation anywhere."

This was something that was beyond the British white blues players—at least until they could get to the United States. Of course by the time they got here, their very successes had changed all the rules. Call and response, the cornerstone of black music, had to be experienced to be believed, much less understood. It was the machinery that created the extraordinary bond between performer and audience, that made each party a participant in a ritual that was already old when America was just being born.

Yet one of the reasons for the white blues kids' acceptance in the blues world was the increasing disfavor in which the blues (and their urban offspring, rhythm and blues) were held in the black community. It was the time of the Great Awakening of the black middle class, and "upwardly mobile" was the byword.

"The blues and R & B were rapidly falling out of favor with the black community," says Norman Dayron, who had quickly risen from janitor to engineer to producer. "Things were upward and mobile and hip, and they didn't want to hear pain, reminders of the old days in the South, guttural accents and primitive sorts of things.

Middle-class blacks were disgusted with the blues, just the same as my parents would have been."

"See, I don't think their own kids were much interested in what their fathers were doing," says Michael Bloomfield of his acceptance by blacks. "It was not just that I was white, but here was a young man who had learned a good deal of this tradition and seemed to want to carry it on, and I think they were only too glad to have a competent musician who wanted to carry on the tradition. Muddy [Waters] told me last time I saw him, only about a year ago, that he was wondering what would happen to the blues when he got too old to play it because of his sons' and children's disinterest in it." (In fact, the white blues kids echoed almost the very words of southern pickers who learned their trade from the bluesmen in Memphis. Said one, who later toured with some of the biggest British blues acts, "The most important thing I've ever done in my life was playing with those men. It sorta cuts both ways—them seeing that me, a white kid, was willing to carry it on meant that their lives weren't in vain. It showed them that what they were doing was worthwhile, because somebody would be around to play it when they were gone.")

The white blues kids were successful, but not *that* successful. In 1965 Elektra Records, looking to break out of its folksy image as producer of such artists as Judy Collins, persuaded Paul Butterfield, who had his own band (which included Elvin Bishop, Jerome Arnold, and Sam Lay), to join forces with Michael Bloomfield to form the Butterfield Blues Band. That band became the first electric band to play the Newport Folk Festival, an act that at once outraged folk purists and established the Butter-

field Blues Band as an instant powerhouse. They immediately topped that by backing Bob Dylan at the same
festival in his first electric set, which shook the rafters of
American music—the sainted Bob Dylan, prince of the
gooey metaphor and darling of the folkies, singing rock
and roll with the white blues kids slamming along right
behind him.

Bloomfield joined Dylan on his *Highway 61 Revisited*
album, an event recorded by Al Kooper, one of the New
York City white blues kids, in his book *Backstage Passes*.
Kooper had talked his way into the session as a reporter
for *Sing Out!,* the folk music magazine, but he'd brought
along his guitar just in case Dylan needed a guitar
player.

"Suddenly Dylan exploded through the doorway, and
in tow was this bizarre-looking guy carrying a Fender
Telecaster guitar *without* a case. Which was weird, because it was the dead of winter and the guitar was all wet
from the snow and rain," wrote Kooper. "But he just
shuffled over into a corner, wiped it off, plugged in and
commenced to play some of the most incredible guitar
I'd ever heard. That's all the Seven Lick Kid [Kooper]
had to hear; I was in over my head. I anonymously un-
plugged, packed up, and did my best to look like a reporter from *Sing Out!* magazine." The bizarre-looking
guy was Michael Bloomfield. Kooper subsequently
formed the Blues Project, the *other* white blues kids
group.

The reason the white blues kids didn't end up fat, rich,
and famous is a matter of some conjecture. They all did
well—some of Butterfield's albums are classics (as is his
performance on the Band's farewell movie, *The Last
Waltz,* where he is so good he is almost scary). Bloomfield,

along with Gravenites and Buddy Miles, formed the Electric Flag, one of the greatest cult bands of the late 1960s, then drifted off to various "supersessions," including his classic with Al Kooper and Stephen Stills, and formed a couple of other bands. Gravenites is in demand as a producer, as is Dayron (he produced two of Chess' best-selling albums, Muddy Waters' *Fathers and Sons* and *The Howlin' Wolf Sessions*). Some say simply that the white blues kids were ahead of their time. Others claim their insistence on a high degree of musical virtuosity made it hard for them to play with anyone but themselves.

But these conventional explanations overlook the fact that the white blues kids had an intrinsic disadvantage compared to their British cousins—they *knew* they were white boys playing the blues, and they were not willing to expropriate the music while explaining how universal it was. They had, as Norman Dayron said, taken on the blues burden. Part of that burden was seeing that their teachers got the respect they deserved. "We got 'em contracts," says Gravenites, who produced two albums of Otis Spann. "And not just 'nigger' contracts, either. We got them more money than they'd ever gotten before in their life." Dayron's albums of Howlin' Wolf and Muddy Waters probably *did* pay these artists more than they'd made in their careers up to that point. Michael Bloomfield personally arranged with promoter Bill Graham for B. B. King to appear before an all-white audience at San Francisco's Fillmore Auditorium, an appearance that helped rocket B. B. to stardom among whites as well as blacks. If you like us, Bloomfield, Butterfield, and the others told their fans, for god's sake listen to the people who taught us everything we know.

In a sense the white blues kids' fanaticism about the

blues protected them from the worst of the White Negro Syndrome. "Well, we used to wear dark sports coats, little stingy-brimmed hats, dark shirts buttoned up to the top, and in the late 1950s and early 1960s anyone who walked around like that maybe had a joint in his pocket, was a gangster of love, a hipster, or a beatnik," says Dayron. "We were proud of it, man. We never discussed it, but it was there."

"We saw people in their lowest state," says Gravenites, and as a result the musicians in the group had fewer illusions about black culture than your run-of-the-mill liberal, who got most of his impressions about black culture from the only aspect of that culture open to him— the music.

"The black society was morally . . . whatever you wanna call it . . . a lot looser than white. There were a lot more ladies, a lot more funky people," states Gravenites, a little bit of the hoodlum still showing after all these years maybe. "The clubs we played in were all wild clubs. People would get really down. We weren't used to that in white society. It just didn't exist in white society. I think that was the main allure—it was a lot more fun."

Bloomfield remembers meeting lots of "white niggers" at that time, almost all of whom hated blacks: "They were the white guys who spoke with a pseudo-black accent and wore black clothes and drove big pimp cars, and I saw that ever since I was a kid. I mean, there were people in Chicago who *hated* blacks, but who had an almost black style in everything they did. . . . I wasn't interested in becoming a white black man. . . . I was always an urban Jew, a very well off urban Jew, and I never wanted to be anything but that. I didn't want to be a white black guy. That wasn't my scene at all."

But as the 1960s ground on, it proved to be a lot of

other people's scene; it's *still* a lot of people's scene. Not everybody would choose to pick up the bluesman's burden.

"We done our duty," Gravenites says, in closing. "Let's put it that way. We done our duty."

ICONS

She was an art form, a source of energy, a way of life in the sixties.
—Critic Ed Naha on Janis Joplin

Jimi Hendrix was the flower generation's nigger dandy—its king stud and golden calf, its maker of mighty dope music, its most outrageous visible force.
—Critic John Morthland on Jimi Hendrix

It was the time of the gods again, and all things were once more possible. The white blues kids had been successful beyond their wildest imagination, the Flower Power generation had already picked up the chant: "Blues . . . blues . . . blues." In 1967, at the Monterey Pop Festival, the many divergent forces working on music in the late 1960s all came together in a series of climactic incidents that changed the face of rock once again.

Amazingly, the changes wrought by Monterey were

197

contradictory. The mass audience—almost exclusively white—got their first real taste of soul music as they were brought to their feet again and again by the master, Otis Redding. Redding was the only soul singer at Monterey, although soul music had been a force to be reckoned with on the popular music scene since the early 1960s. Otis sang soul, and the audience's heart melted away.

But when the mist cleared from their eyes, the audience didn't want to hear *soul.* They wanted the *blues.* And they got the blues with a vengeance from the white blues kids to the Grateful Dead. The person who really stole the show, though, was a white blues singer from Port Arthur, Texas, named Janis Joplin.

By the time of the Monterey festival Joplin was a fixture in San Francisco's psychedelic revolution, a refugee from the Texas hill country. She'd begun singing in Port Arthur—a hopeless situation if there ever was one—and had run away from home at the age of seventeen in 1960. While on the road she discoverd a blues album by Leadbelly, perhaps the most famous of the traveling singers of the 1930s and 1940s, and that record changed her life. She began searching out blues and found Odetta and classic works by Bessie Smith. When she began singing again, what came out was the blues.

After drifting around Texas for a while she was caught up in the tidal pull to the West Coast, and in 1966 settled in San Francisco and took a job as vocalist for one of that area's many cult bands, Big Brother and the Holding Company. They were still a little shaky around the edges when they walked onto the stage at Monterey. When they walked off the stage they were superstars, complete with a shiny new recording contract.

The third part of the Monterey Triangle was a black

guitar player named James Marshall Hendrix, who, in a few minutes onstage, managed to totally rewrite the way rock guitar was played. "Jimi did a beautiful Spade routine," wrote the underground *East Village Other.* "Socked it to them." "Hendrix is a psychedelic Uncle Tom," sniffed *Esquire's* new "modern" music critic. "He was terrible." The crowd went bonkers.

Of the three, the odyssey of James Marshall (Jimi) Hendrix is perhaps the strangest. He grew up in middle-class Seattle with a so-so interest in the blues and the grimy life on the road that such an interest entailed. After a stretch in the Army Hendrix went on the chitlin' circuit, backing up everybody from B. B. King (his idol) to Wilson Pickett to the Isley Brothers. He reached a turning point in the mid-1960s when he first heard Bob Dylan. Hendrix had always had serious reservations about his voice (which wasn't so hot), but after hearing Dylan's voice (which also wasn't so hot), he decided to strike out on his own.

Dylan influenced Hendrix on an even deeper level, giving the black guitarist a permanent affection for deep (some say abstruse) lyrics fraught with symbolism. Hendrix went to New York City's Greenwich Village—where Dylan started—and began making the rounds with blues bands, most of which were white. Eventually he worked with his own group, Jimmy James and the Blue Flames, and was "discovered" by Chas Chandler of the Animals, who persuaded Hendrix to come to England and become a star.

The reason Hendrix had to go to England to become a star was that he was pushing the boundaries of rock music further and further toward the weird, utilizing fuzz, feedback, and just plain skill. He was no longer playing the blues, although the blues contributed much to what he played. Chas Chandler theorized that once Jimi had been "Englandized," turned into a strutting Mod peacock, he would be readily acceptable to the American audience. Monterey proved Chandler right.

Although the times had changed dramatically, the basic feelings of the record-buying audience had not. Blacks could only be accepted on terms strictly defined by the "rock" establishment. Jimmy James and the Blue Flames would be relegated to the chitlin' circuit, making a few bucks a night and reaching a totally black audience. Jimi Hendrix and the Experience, however (the Experience being two white journeymen players from England, Noel Redding and Mitch Mitchell), were totally acceptable to whites. It was the old British Invasion line—he's not black; he's *English!*

This is not to imply that Hendrix didn't expand the horizons of rock. He did, and his guitar echoes are still making the rounds, but he served an additional function that Monterey mate Otis Redding could never serve, that of the acceptable black stud. As critic John Morthland wrote in the *Rolling Stone Illustrated History of Rock and Roll,* he was a nigger dandy.

Ironically, Hendrix's professional blackness eventually turned into a deadly two-edged sword. Jimi Hendrix's audience, almost always predominantly white, was unwilling to accept a black man fronting for a white group (the Stax and Muscle Shoals rhythm sections, largely white, had wisely chosen to remain in the background, leaving the spotlight solely on the soul men). There was increasing pressure from his fans and from the increasingly militant (at least rhetorically) black musicians for Hendrix to dump the Experience and form an all-black band. In 1969 Hendrix broke his ties with Chandler, disbanded the Experience, and formed the all-black Band of Gypsies, featuring Buddy Miles on drums and Billy Cox on bass. The Band of Gypsies had a short, fitful existence. Try as he might, Hendrix never could find the magic again, and he died on September 18, 1970, of complications resulting from a barbiturate overdose.

For Janis Joplin, the road from Monterey to death by drug overdose in October of 1970 was equally rocky and covered much the same ground. She had, in essence, picked up the torch from the white blues kids, the bluesman's burden. She was, as she told everybody within earshot, a blues singer. Not a *white* blues singer, not a white girl singing the blues, but the next step on the evolutionary ladder; from spirituals to gospel to blues to rhythm and blues to rock to her. The beat had been passed to the next generation, and Janis Joplin was holding the torch.

And she was one hell of a singer, the possessor of a thunderous voice that could perhaps rival the voices of some of the ladies who sang the blues in the old days. She became increasingly obsessed with the idea of the blues, though, and the melancholy that went with that music. People had to understand, she told a newspaper interviewer in San Francisco in the late 1960s, that it was the white kids now who were carrying the torch. The blacks used to have it, she said, and now it was hers. In 1968 she went to Memphis, to the annual Stax Records Review, to cement her crown.

On that particular night near Christmas the air in the auditorium was sweet with the smells of good times and soul music, and had the right preacher shown up, I'm sure we'd all have been saved. For four or five hours the best black singers in America had filed onto the stage of the old auditorium, trying to turn the audience into a dancing, quivering mass of excited humanity. There were Rufus and Carla Thomas, Arthur Conley, Wilson Pickett, Eddie Floyd, Sam and Dave, Isaac Hayes, and special guest James Brown, the Godfather of Soul himself. At the end of the bill was a special added attraction—Janis Joplin.

There were very few white faces in the crowd of thirteen thousand; in fact, before the lights went down, I counted three, aside from my own. The only other white faces were in the band, Booker T. and the M.G.'s, the house band at Stax. (It was something of a local joke that the best black rhythm section in the world was half-white—Steve Cropper and Duck Dunn, rounding out Al Jackson and Booker T. himself.)

The show was beyond words, a cross between a passionate love affair and a roll-around-on-the-floor revival meeting, and by midnight we were all near exhaustion. My friend Martin was so overcome that he was finally able to take his hand off the knife in his pocket, which he had brought along to protect himself in this Valley of the Shadow of Death. After a couple of dozen encores by everybody, the house lights went down again and a frail-looking white girl walked onstage carrying a fifth of whiskey. She went up to the microphone, took a hit off the bottle, and said, "Hi-ya." There was a smattering of applause, a few knowing glances exchanged. Then she launched into "Ball and Chain," and it was clear what Janis Joplin was attempting to do. The acknowledged queen of the white blues singers had come to Memphis to remove the adjective of color from her title. She had come to Memphis defiantly, to throw her color in the

face of this exhausted crowd who'd done everything short
of crawling on their knees for Carla Thomas, the woman
they called the Queen of Soul. Think white people can't
sing the blues, she told this black audience. Well, listen to
this, Memphis!

Wrong crowd, wrong night, wrong town. The crowd
wasn't having any honky bullshit. There were rumbles
that were clearly not applause. Janis was singing wonder-
fully, but she was simply no match for the intensity of
what had passed before her. The call-and-response electricity simply wasn't there. She had nothing to tell that
particular crowd about the blues, because they had lived
and eaten and slept with the blues; they knew the way
the blues tasted, felt, and smelled. The electricity passing
through the audience was all wrong, exactly the opposite
of the blues feeling. The singer seemed to be commu-
nicating that she had a *right* to sing the blues. The audience became overtly hostile—*When you say you got a right
to sing the blues, then you and me ain't talkin' about the same
blues.* Those white guys onstage never said anything
about rights; they just got up there and played what was
inside them, without analysis, hand wringing, or hype,
and what came out was the blues—soul music.

She finished her first number, and there was a smattering of applause. Most of the audience had already
headed for the exits. She did one more number, then
stopped abruptly. If you don't want to listen, she said,
then I'm going to leave.

And she walked offstage in a blind fury, still the best
white blues singer there was. The boys in the band shook
their heads. Martin and I got out in one piece, although
it was touch and go for a couple of minutes—when the
music's over, the real world has a way of coming back

with a vengeance. The next morning the local newspaper mentioned that Miss Joplin was upset by the audience's lack of response.

The icons of the 1960s died with the decade, and their legacy was a mixed one. The question of race remained unresolved, for the rock audience remained doggedly inconsistent on the issue. While Redding was clearly the best performer of the three, and Hendrix's the most powerful musical contribution, it was Janis Joplin who ultimately had the greatest effect. She ushered in the age of the white nigger, riding close on the heels of the politicalization of rock in the late 1960s. As waves of unrest swept the campuses, white middle-class kids sought some way to define their new consciousness, their new political leanings. Much of the rhetoric had been adopted in the early years of the 1960s from the civil rights movement, but it was a self-conscious, even embarrassed, adoption. In the late 1960s the kids finally found the groove, thanks to the pioneering successes of the British blues bands and the white blues kids. With the canonization of Janis Joplin, the white nigger could become a reality.

BULLDOZING
THE NIGGERS

Listen to that rock music, which provides the kids with their phraseology, their philosophy, their life-style, the ideas and attitudes that motivate them and with which they explain the world.
—The Kumquat Statement:
Anarchy in the Groves of Academe,
by John R. Coyne, Jr.

To the cops, we're all niggers.
—A Lower East Side organizer, quoted in
The Strawberry Statement: Notes of a College Revolutionary
by James Simon Kunen

I can't recall the exact moment when I figured out that I could grow up to be a nigger, but I do remember the concept swelling my head until it was almost ready to burst. A nigger! A *nig-ger!* Won't my parents be surprised! Won't my friends be impressed! There I'll be, out there on some picket line or leafleting to smash the state (avoiding my 7:30 a.m. French class, which is okay because the teacher realizes that I'm a *nigger*, and we *niggers* got things to do), and some other *nigger*, a real black guy, maybe, with a foxy black chick on his arm, will come cruising by and stop to make *nigger* talk with me. He'll give me *five*, and I'll give 'em right back, and he'll say, "Rite on, bro' (that's *nigger* talk for *brother*, get it?). Powah to dah pee-pulh!"

Only by the time I was in college, I didn't know any blacks anymore. Blacks kept to themselves, and so did whites. Beale Street, with its lazy ambiance and its snake-quick flashes of violence, was half a country away, rotting in the sullen winter sunshine and half-remembered memories of better times. In the largely white world of the universities of the late 1960s, to be black was to be hip beyond any question. To be black was to be a member of an exclusive secret club, founded in the bloody iron of shackles and reborn in the smoking ghettoes and at the end of a redneck sheriff's billy club. To be black was to speak a secret language, wear funny clothes from Africa, and be able to talk about "the revolution" and not sound like a total jerk. We white boys were green with envy.

True, there was the civil rights movement; there was the Vietnam War; there were things *wrong* with America, and a lot of kids took to the streets in those strange times in the earnest belief that taking to the streets would right those wrongs. But if patriotism remains the last refuge of a scoundrel, idealism provides the same haven for the naïve. Much of what happened in the 1960s and early 1970s was a vast effort on the part of a lot of white middle-class kids to become *anything* other than white and middle class. The culture was changing—every song on the radio said so. Not AM radio, for heaven's sake. *That was still stuck on Ray Stevens singing "Everything Is Beautiful.*" But FM radio had the Rolling Stones on the Street Fighting Man; or Eric Burden on the Sky Pilot (too heavy for AM, all right); or the Doors on sex, death, and violence; or the Jefferson Airplane, once those hopeless Flower Children from San Francisco, singing about (dare we say it?) *revolution.*

Revolution; riot; demonstration; *nigger*—the words roll over the tongue like that first glass of under-eighteen beer. Sweet words, forbidden words, words that washed away all the things our mommies and our daddies had planned for us. We would be revolutionaries, but before we could become revolutionaries (Hey, Che, whatda'ya say?), we had to become *niggers.*

And why *couldn't* we be niggers? After all, we already had the blues.

Ask any voodoo doctor, sometimes words have got the power. More than sticks and stones, some words have the power to break or mend, to shatter or put back together again. "Nigger" is such a word. It carries the weight of three centuries of hatred, like some cosmic snowball with a boulder in the middle. People have died over the use of that particular word, and there are places in the United States today—this very afternoon—where its injudicious use can get you a knife blade stuffed up to your breastbone. It is a word that the white man invented to describe the black man, an ugly word that can't be said without spitting it out, as if the flavor of it offended the tongue. Nigger, nigger, nigger, nigger, nigger, nigger, said comedian Lenny Bruce, keep saying it until the word has no *power.* So far, nobody's been able to say it enough times for that.

The concept of the White Negro was hardly new. Jack

Kerouac had written in *On the Road* that he wished he was a Negro, and Norman Mailer was expostulating on the subject just about the time the white blues kids were really getting into ghetto life. But with the growth of the "Counterculture" in the late 1960s the idea began whipping around the nation's campuses like wildfire.

They were primed and ready for it, thanks to the British Invasion and the workings of the white blues kids. Black culture was still about as alien as the dark side of the moon, but whites had co-opted (not stolen) the music. By the late 1960s white blues players, both the seemingly indestructible British bands and the numerous clones of the white blues kids, had a hammerlock on high-energy rock and roll, which was the only music suitable for a revolution. Both Motown and Stax soul music were on their last legs and fading fast, and the replacement black music was super-Motown from Philadelphia. Blacks, it seemed, weren't all that interested in smashing the state—the Kerner Commission on Civil Disorders, for example, found that black protests throughout the 1960s were aimed more at getting a fair piece of the pie than throwing the pie in somebody's face. So while white music—white blues, if you will—continued in the smash-the-beer-bottle tradition of the bars (modified to suit the changing lyrical tastes of its ever-expanding and increasingly politicized market), black music got straighter and straighter, dressed nicer, and kept practicing those dance steps. If the white folks were going to sing about revolution, somebody had to be around to keep dancing.

Nobody was around to record when the first student decided he was a nigger, although the closest anyone could come to dating the turning point would be the Democratic Convention in Chicago in the summer of

1968. It stood to reason that normal, run-of-the-mill white kids from nice homes and good universities would hardly get smacked over the head with a club by a Chicago cop, so those cops must be at least *thinking* they were hitting something else. Like niggers. Niggers *always* get hit over the head.

The idea took root with incredible speed. If you were a little dense, there was a pamphlet that made the rounds (although I've been unable to find a copy of it) called "The Student as Nigger" that detailed how a student, who was paying a lot of money to go to an institute of higher learning and who viewed anything less than $15,000-a-year salary as hardly worth the effort, could mentally equate himself with a field hand. I recall the pamphlet was immensely popular. The fault was not entirely that of the students. Liberal and radical intellectuals and politicians, anxious to jump on the bandwagon before there was no room for them, were more than willing to lump students and blacks into the same bushel basket. One-time presidential candidate and representative from New York Shirley Chisholm, a black woman, declared in 1969 that "eventually a coalition of college students and black people will save American society." One academic tract written that year characterized the students as the "New Class" and described in glowing terms the New Class' inevitable alliance with the "Underclass," that is, the blacks.

The most powerful black voices of the time, especially the radical black voices, were anxious to cement a bond between the growing student movement and the newly refired Black Power movement. "The fourth stage, now in its infancy, sees these white youths taking the initiative, using techniques learned in the Negro struggle to attack problems in the general society," wrote Eldridge Cleaver in *Soul on Ice.* "The characteristics of the white rebels which most alarm their elders—the long hair, the new dances, their love for Negro music, their use of marijuana, their mystical attitude toward sex—are all the tools of their rebellion." Most of those characteristics came directly from the white kids' perceptions of black culture!

Long hair we'll kick back to the Beatles (Ha! See that connection?), but the strange dances have their roots in Africa, the use of "killer weed" was lifted straight from the black blues and jazz clubs, and the "mystical" viewpoint of sex—that you should be able to do it lots and lots without having to get married or feel guilty—came straight from the lyrics of that Negro music the students liked.

No *wonder* white kids started thinking they were niggers—half the country was telling them they were. So it's great to call everybody brother and sister (just be careful not to call any black guys in the ghetto "brother" lest you end up chewing a blade), it's okay to get down and boogie, talk some trash, and get a little nookie. Well, better hold up on the nookie, since John Lennon has revealed that "woman is the nigger of the world," which effectively supersedes the Black Panther concept that a woman's place in the "revolution" is prone.

We can't overlook the liberal guilt factor in the niggerization of the universities. While the kids were listening to the radio, a lot of their liberal parents were wringing their hands trying to figure out what to do. "White liberals," said S. I. Hayakawa, the scourge of the University of California, "in their hunger for humiliation, will take as revealed truth anything an angry black man says."

About the time the most thoroughly niggerized white kids were talking about "picking up the gun" for a genuine let-the-blood-flow-in-the-streets rebellion, it ended, as if somebody had reached out and thrown a switch. Demonstrations were suddenly tasteless, revolution gauche, we were all getting older and facing the prospect of, God forbid, working.

But we didn't forget how neat it felt when we were all niggers, and in 1971, miraculously, we turned on our radios and heard the wave of the future. The song was called "Shaft," the soundtrack from a movie of the same name. The movie was one of a budding genre called blaxploitation, and we ate that up! No more having to listen to song lyrics to find out what's happen'n, man, just go to the movies and get *soul,* subclass *blue-eyed.* The music for those movies came from Memphis, but it was unlike any music Memphis had ever produced before. The man of the hour was Isaac Hayes, and he had reached out and fused the soul he'd learned at Stax with the butter-smooth arrangements he'd heard from Motown. The result was funky music you could dance to—the birth of for-real disco music.

So now we had the music for the next decade, the Me Decade, but we were still a little short on style. Funky Negro was out, and nothing had as yet come in. The door to the saloon was kicked open the very next year in the form of another blaxploitation movie. This movie wasn't nearly as slick as *Shaft,* but the music, by Curtis Mayfield, was oh so good.

And the main character—what a man! He was black, but he took shit from nobody—not the black militants, not the white pigs, not the mob. He did his thing, and he was black and beautiful. His name was Superfly and he dealt cocaine, an honorable profession in the concrete jungle. When Ron O'Neal, decked out in a Superfly white suit, driving a Superfly pimpmobile, cruised onto that screen, with Curtis Mayfield's theme wailing in the background, the 1970s were *really* born.

Shee-it, man, I'm gonna get rid of these jeans and get me some *threads,* and I be *bad,* like that dude Superfly. If we couldn't be Funky Negro, then we'd be Superfly.

THE GOOD OLE BOYS

Southern rock, at its best, is something more than rock that happens to be played in the South. . . . Today's Southern rock . . . is essentially an attempt to recreate and refine some of the original fusions in a modern-day setting.

—Frye Gaillard in *Watermelon Wine*

This ain't no fashion show; we came here to play.

—Duane Allman

The air in Atlanta was thick enough to cut with a butter knife, and the 600,000 or so folks lounging around the cow pasture couldn't do anything except take off their clothes and pray for the sun to set. It was the second Atlanta Pop Festival—Woodstock South—and it was 1970, the summer after the original Woodstock. All things were possible.

After suffering through set after set of people no one in

their right mind would pay money to hear, the crowd began murmuring and shuffling like some huge hairy animal just waking up, rubbing its thousands of eyes at the setting sun and waiting for the Allman Brothers Band to make everything all right. While the rest of the country might not yet have any idea who these long-haired country boys were, to the teeming city in the cow pasture, they were already heroes, the pride of south Georgia.

The Allman Brothers Band—Duane and Gregg Allman, Richard Betts, Berry Oakley, Butch Trucks, and Jaimoe Johanson—had materialized out of thin air to take the South by storm, playing a music that had almost nothing to do with what was popular at the time. Motown still dominated the charts, and everything that wasn't Motown was either the Archies or Tony Orlando and Dawn. But the Allman Brothers' music was something else, a mean, bluesy, visceral blend of the South's two greatest exports—the blues and country music. It was music that rang bells most people had forgotten they had.

The band ambled onto the stage like a group of guys who just happened to wander by and see the instruments. Nothing fancy—no natty clothes or matching outfits. No Motown stage routines or witty patter, just a simple introduction that had practically become the band's trademark: "We're the Allman Brothers Band from Macon, Georgia, and we came here to play."

And play they did, for about the next eight hours, all through the long Georgia night until a sliver of dawn appeared on the horizon. Even through my befuddled eyes I could see that this was something special, something that transcended the idea of "concert." While they played, the more established stars on the bill—people like

Johnny Winter, already pegged by *Rolling Stone* magazine as the Next Big Thing, and the sainted Jimi Hendrix— made their way to the stage to be a part of the magic, to match their guitars against the soaring dual leads of Duane Allman and Richard Betts.

Within a few months the band would go to New York City to record *Live at the Fillmore East,* which would establish the Brothers as a major force in rock music and would be referred to, many years later, by one critic as a "spooky pinnacle" in the history of rock and roll. A few months after that Duane Allman would be killed in a motorcycle accident, as would Berry Oakley a year later. And the band would go on until, by 1974, it was the premier American rock and roll band.

Southern rock has remained, through thick and thin, one of the major musical influences of the 1970s. In fact, southern rock, as promulgated by groups such as the Allman Brothers and the Marshall Tucker Band, as well as such left-field additions as the Outlaws, the Elvin Bishop Band, Charlie Daniels, and the country branch of the family, which includes such Nashville luminaries as Waylon Jennings and Hank Williams, Jr., forms one of the three legs of 1970s music, the other two being disco and West Coast "soft" rock.

Even at the very height of the New Wave media storm in the summer of 1979, one of the biggest hits was veteran good ole boy Charlie Daniels' "The Devil Went Down to Georgia," a song that managed to be a hit on AM radio, FM radio, and country radio without so much as a how-y'all-doin' to tastemakers and critics everywhere.

Southern rock has been an unwanted stepchild almost

from the first day the Allman Brothers hit the road in the late 1960s. Critics who got on the southern rock bandwagon in the late 1970s were quick to jump off when New Wave (*née* punk) offered itself as a critical alternative. The reasons are pretty straightforward. One, southern rock, as practiced by such groups as the Brothers, the Marshall Tucker Band, the Charlie Daniels Band, the Outlaws, the late Lynyrd Skynyrd, and many others living and deceased, began as a rural southern phenomenon, and critics tend to see only the urban Northeast or California. Two, the nature of southern music, with its extended guitar jams and emphasis on bluesy or country vocals, is ill-suited to Top 40 radio, which has always shot for the biggest possible audience, which is to be had by offending as few people as humanly possible. It was the huge, overpowering successes of the southern bands as tour attractions that *forced* their records onto the radio. The Marshall Tucker Band, for example, was routinely told by station programmers that their records were "too rock" to be played on country stations and "too country" to be played on rock stations, a situation that persisted right up until the Tuckers began routinely drawing crowds of fifteen and twenty thousand at each concert. Three, the "tastemakers," publications like *Rolling Stone, The Village Voice* in New York City, *Creem* magazine in Detroit, and other heavy members of the rock press, didn't take to the style or attitude of the groups. The southern bands owed their success to the masses, and the tastemakers have never been comfortable with popular choices. (Both Creedence Clearwater Revival and the Doors, for example, were castigated by critics because they had hit singles, which were perceived as less morally pure than artistic albums that failed commercially. In retrospect it can be seen that the two groups produced some of the finest radio rock ever done.) The ultimate reason for the success of southern rock is that it represents the most recent fusion of black and white, and it shows once again how powerful that fusion can be.

"It grew, the musicians tell you, out of black rhythm and blues and white country and western," wrote the *Richmond Times Dispatch* in a 1974 newspaper article, "music of the out-back radio stations and dance halls of the rural South. It owes its character not to Bill Haley and Elvis Presley, but to Otis Redding and Merle Haggard."

It's all a question, say Jerry Eubanks and George McCorkle of the Marshall Tucker Band, of where you were raised. "We were raised in the South," says Eubanks. "You grow up listening to rhythm and blues and country music, and that's what you learn."

The various members of the Tucker Band grew up in Spartanburg, South Carolina, and have worked together as a band since junior high school. Perhaps more than any other group to come out of Dixie in recent years, the Tucker Band has managed to remain close to its roots. Their music includes a healthy dose of the blues and bar funk—that ubiquitous get-up-and-dance bar music that seems to flow just beneath the surface of southern life—with an equal helping of Hank Williams' patented country despair, along with some jazz and Western Swing on the side.

"It's like this," says George McCorkle, with the magic age of thirty already behind him. "After a while you get older and your music matures. You start playing your roots, whether it's country or blues or whatever. It's what you grew up with, and you can't escape it."

The music might have remained a southern anomaly had it not been for an ex-high school fraternity boy named Phil Walden, a white boy who became the manager and close personal friend of Otis Redding; who was the biggest booker and manager of soul acts in the country; who discovered Duane Allman playing sessions guitar in Muscle Shoals and urged him to form his own band; who launched his own record company, Capricorn, in Macon, Georgia, which, during the decade of the 1970s, dominated southern music and which, Phil Walden claims, will rise again in the 1980s.

The saga of Capricorn Records is deeply rooted in Phil Walden's unswerving southern chauvinism. "Southern culture is unique," he has said over and over again to anyone who would listen. "Southerners should be damn proud of being southerners, whether they're black or white." Capricorn rose from its unlikely beginnings to become the largest and most successful independent label in the country, as well as a major force in American music. In its heyday in the mid-1970s Capricorn was earning around $44 million a year and was spreading the gospel of southern music with all the fire and enthusiasm of a backwoods tent revivalist. Not content with spreading southern music, Walden engineered a series of concerts with southern acts to promote presidential candidate Jimmy Carter, a close personal friend. The concerts, which netted almost half a million dollars (a sum that was matched by federal election funds), were a stroke of genius. Each ticketholder became an official contributor to the Carter campaign, and insiders say the Capricorn money arrived just as the fledgling campaign was beginning to feel the financial pinch; some even credit the money with saving the campaign. When Carter reportedly asked Walden what he wanted in return, Walden replied, "A southerner in the White House."

Oddly enough, the small town of Macon, Georgia (population: around 100,000), was already a hotbed of musical activity. Richard Penniman, better known to the world as Little Richard, washed dishes in the Greyhound Bus Station in Macon while he was working on the song that would make him a star, "Tutti Frutti." When he hit big, Phil Walden became his biggest fan.

"He was on the first rock and roll show I ever went to see," Walden says. "He used to play around here in a place I couldn't get into—a very rough bar. I wasn't old enough to get in."

Three days after hearing "Tutti Frutti" on the radio for the first time, ninth-grader Walden spotted Little Richard strutting down the street, carrying an umbrella.

"Tutti frutti!" Walden yelled across the street.

"All rutti!" Little Richard screamed back. The two went on to become friends.

Both James Brown and Otis Redding also hailed from Macon, and both worked the sleazy little clubs around town waiting for the same break that had catapulted Richard Penniman to stardom.

For Phil Walden, the discovery of black music was a revelation. He was born in 1940 in South Carolina, and moved with his family to Macon when he was three years old. Life went along pretty normally until about the eighth grade, when an older brother who had moved to Indiana to work returned to Macon for a visit.

"He brought back this stack of 78 rpm records and a record player," Walden says. "They were all groups like the Coasters or Big Joe Turner or Hank Ballard and the Midnighters. I thought it was just incredible. It was the greatest music I had ever heard. I was so used to hearing the lily-white, watered-down doo-wop on the radio that this music was really something special. It was so earthy. . . . It had a rawness that really appealed to me."

Walden began pouring over the "black society" page in the local newspaper, looking for notices of appearances by black bands. To his surprise, he found that the music he loved was all around Macon, there for the taking. His first discovery was Little Richard.

While a quick comparison to the white blues kids seems in order, the analogy doesn't quite hold. The biggest difference is the music itself—southern music, as we saw in earlier chapters, has a real knack for becoming a bastardization of itself. While a southern enclave in Chicago might support a blues colony, music in the South was constantly shifting, always moving toward the ubiquitous black-and-white bar music. The three pillars of Macon black music—Little Richard, James Brown, and Otis Redding—represent three distinct approaches to black music, and no one of the three is nearly as "pure" black as, say, Muddy Waters. Little Richard is rhythm and blues filtered through the rockabilly madness of Elvis Presley; James Brown is unsanctified gospel, which would eventually be filtered through keen observation of the British Invasion (Brown was the first black artist to successfully package and market the Real Thing in response to the wave of British imitation); and, of course, Otis Redding was soul music, which, as we have seen, owes as much to white as to black.

A second fault in the analogy is the inescapable presence of blacks in the South. You didn't need to take a trip to the South Side ghettoes in order to find blacks—you could see Little Richard walking down the main street of

Macon. Blacks were not so much alien as different. This is not to say that black culture wasn't attractive to young southern whites, because it was, and for pretty much the same reasons that it appealed to the white blues kids in Chicago. But in the cities of the South that culture was much more visible and accessible.

Walden was hooked on the music, and pretty soon he was booking bands at high school fraternity dances and sock hops. A shot at his own band, with him as the lead singer, flopped—"no talent"—so Walden consoled himself by managing a band called the Heartbreakers. Every Saturday morning he trundled his charges down to the Greyhound Bus Station, where one of the band members worked, to practice in the baggage area for that day's talent show at a black theater across the street. Since whites weren't allowed in the theater, Walden would shoo his charges into the theater and then race back to his car in the parking lot to listen to the show on the radio. And every week the Heartbreakers kept coming in second to a local singer named Otis "Rockhouse" Redding, who would come out and sing an Elvis Presley song and blow the house away.

"I figured I'd better meet this guy," Walden says.

Soon Walden, by now a sophomore at Mercer College in Macon, was booking Otis Redding around town as the singer for Little Willie Jones and the Mighty Panthers. Walden had even managed to open an "office," a nine-by-twelve-foot space with a flat black Army surplus desk and a telephone, the walls coverd with pictures of artists Walden could only dream about meeting, much less representing—"for inspiration."

"I used to answer the phone in this little falsetto voice—'Hold on please. Mr. Walden is on the other line,' " Walden says, laughing. "There *wasn't* any other line, just like there wasn't a secretary."

One of Walden's recent acquisitions was a popular local group called Johnny Jenkins and the Pinetoppers, and when that group got a shot at an audition at Stax Records in Memphis, Walden jumped at the chance.

"We'd cut this single in Atlanta called 'Miss Thing,' which got changed to 'Love Twist,' and a local deejay played the living hell out of it," Walden says. "So we decided to go to Memphis. I rented a station wagon, but since I was still in college, I couldn't go. So I hired Otis to drive it, since Johnny Jenkins couldn't drive. I told Otis, 'If there's any chance at all, when they get through with Johnny, get them to cut a couple of sides on you.' "

That particular session at Stax Records has been enshrined in rock and roll history. After a dud of a session by the Pinetoppers, "Rockhouse" Redding cut "Hey Hey Hey" and "These Arms of Mine" in forty minutes. It took nine months to break "These Arms of Mine" as a hit, but when it went on the charts, both Walden and Redding were beside themselves: "A record on the chart! Man we'd made it. I was in heaven, I was a big-time manager—Colonel Tom Parker, step aside. Otis and I sat down one night and discussed what it might be like to make $10,000 a year. That seemed like such an incredible sum."

The relationship between Walden and Redding had been steadily deepening, until the two had come to regard each other as brothers. Walden's brother Alan bought a farm next door to the Redding farm so the Waldens and the Reddings could get together for hunting and fishing and socializing. Phil's father had become increasingly involved with Otis' career, going on the road with him to take tickets and handle the millions of details a road trip involves.

"Otis literally turned my father from being an old-fashioned southern man who didn't call black people black people . . . Otis turned him completely around," Walden remembers. "I saw my father slap a very prominent Macon businessman in our offices once when that man asked my father, 'How do you put up with all these niggers?' My daddy slapped the living hell out of him, and he said, 'Don't you ever say that word in my presence again.' "

When either of the Walden brothers toured with Otis, they refused to bow to segregationist law, which resulted more often than not in the group being turned away from white hotels for having blacks in their group and from black hotels for having whites in their group.

After Walden finished a twenty-two-month stint in the Army he discovered that his agency had grown to be the largest booker of black talent in the country, thanks largely to the Walden brothers' insistence on honesty. "We were either honest enough or naïve enough to be honest," he says ruefully.

Blacks got paid (something of a novelty) because concert promoters who didn't pay found themselves blackballed and hounded by Walden. Pretty soon the Walden agency was handling the likes of Sam and Dave, Eddie Floyd, Arthur Conley, Clarence Carter, Percy Sledge, Al Green, and Johnny Taylor. Along with the folks in Memphis, Walden masterminded the tremendously successful Stax/Volt European tours and became one of the kingpins in soul music of the mid-1960s.

Then Otis Redding died in a plane crash. He had just finished a widely heralded appearance at the Monterey

Pop Festival in 1967 that had, for the first time, established him solidly with the white market, and his latest release, "Dock of the Bay," was already on the charts. After his death it rose on the charts to become his only No. 1 song.

Walden was shattered. "It was," he says, "a unique relationship, and it was the type of relationship I don't think I can have again."

The death of Redding soured Walden on the soul scene, which was already showing signs of collapsing under the continuous onslaught of Motown and the white blues spinoffs. He began listening to white rock, in particular a sessions guitarist in Muscle Shoals by the name of Duane Allman. Allman had sparkled on cuts by Wilson Pickett (including "Hey Jude") and Aretha Franklin ("It's ironic that on those Aretha sessions, which are considered to be some of the finest black music ever, Aretha is practically the only black there"). At the urging of Atlantic president and southern music afficionado Jerry Wexler, Walden signed Allman and launched his own record label, Capricorn (both Walden's and Wexler's astrological sign), to showcase the new Allman Brothers Band.

"People would come up and ask me how could white people play that way," says Walden of the Allman Brothers' success. "Well, that's the only damn way they can play! They can't play Bach and 'Sentimental Journey,' that's not a reflection of their culture. Somebody asked Duane why, when he was growing up in Daytona Beach, he and Gregg were always playing in black bands. Duane said, 'White kids surf; black kids play music.' They never thought anything about it, being in black bands. Gregg sings like a black guy—well, that's the only damn way he knows how to sing. He can't sing like Frank Sinatra, he's not from New Jersey."

The music of the Allman Brothers—and, ultimately, of all southern rock groups—perfectly reflects the central tension in the South, that tension between black and white. Duane and Gregg grew up in Florida listening to rockabilly and the blues, hard blues like Elmore James, Sonny Boy Williamson, and Howlin' Wolf. Richard Betts, on the other hand, grew up in the rural community of Oneca, Florida, listening to and playing some country music and bluegrass, drifting through Chuck Berry and Elvis Presley as he got older. The other members of the band were equally mixed: Jaimoe, the band's black drummer, toured with Otis Redding and worked in the sophisticated New Orleans R & B scene; Butch Trucks was more into jazz, and bassist Oakley was straight-ahead rock and roll.

Beneath the Allmans' (and later Gregg alone) electrified bar blues, there's always the slightest hint of a bluegrass guitar, a reminder that blue skies are just ahead. And beneath even the most folksy of Richard Betts' compositions are the underlying pain and despair of the blues. And somewhere between those two poles of black and white, blues and country, lies the very soul of the South.

It is, as Frye Gaillard wrote in *Watermelon Wine,* a fine book on country music, a redefining of the original fusion, and after all these years the hybrid offspring is still as strong as a mule.

"I think we suffered from a mentality that we were taught, and that the rest of the country told us we were," says Walden. "The southern white man and the southern black man have always enjoyed a more personal relationship than anyone outside the South thought."

Here the ground gets rocky, because of the fear of being damned as a racist, a legacy of the "New" New South. The relationship between black and white has changed in the South, and not all the changes have been for the better. "I've seen a great deterioration of black culture," says the man who managed Otis Redding, "and that's not to say that the culture should be preserved by racist laws, either. But when we tried to jell everybody together, to make everybody the same, the social shock was just too great. See, southern music has always been a more accurate reflection of southern culture, and southern culture is the most unique culture in the country. It's the one region that still has its own identity, and southerners should be proud of being southerners, black or white."

The saga of Capricorn Records is unfinished. The Allman Brothers fell apart in 1976 in a vicious court battle over drugs, and rumors began circulating later of financial trouble within the ranks of Capricorn. In 1979 Capricorn declared bankruptcy, but not before the Allman Brothers Band managed to stage one of the niftiest comebacks in the history of rock. Right in the middle of the New Wave hype, while critics sniffed that the Brothers were too old, out of touch, and yesterday's news, the band reformed, cut a wildly successful album, and went on a triumphant standing-room-only tour, with tickets to the concerts selling out within a couple of hours of going on sale. They played straight-ahead southern music, and people turned out by the tens of thousands to prove the critics wrong. What they said bears repeating. "We're the Allman Brothers Band from Macon, Georgia, and we came to play."

MODERN MUSIC
(ON THE RADIO)

Disco is the triumph of Motown over Stax.

—Disco disc jockey

The best rock still aspires to tap the temper of its times.
—*The Rolling Stone Illustrated
History of Rock and Roll*

Change comes slowly to the South, and when the change comes, it is seldom as drastic as reported. Southern music, for example, has never lost touch with its roots, no matter how far afield it has strayed. But once the safe confines of the South are left behind, it becomes increasingly harder to make head or tail of music in the 1970s, because the roots are not always apparent, and in some cases there aren't any roots at all.

One of the major reasons a hodgepodge of musical

styles and forms emerged in the 1970s is the very size of the music business. The stakes have risen dramatically. In a penny-ante poker game one might be tempted to draw to an inside straight, flouting the gods and the odds. Raise the stakes to a thousand dollars a bet, or a hundred thousand dollars, and one becomes more cautious. The music business has become high-stakes poker of the headiest sort, with the winners living in baronial estates and driving white Rolls-Royces, while the losers do whatever it is that losers do.

The effects on the music have been twofold. First, there are fewer little guys, independents, than there used to be, and most of those that exist do so under the protection (and usually control) of a major label. The record companies are not solely to blame for this. The public's taste has grown increasingly more sophisticated, and sophistication costs money. Records from the 1950s and 1960s are said to sound "quaint," and the quaintness stems from the fact that they were made cheaply. A slightly humorous aside: In the mid-1970s superstar Bruce Springsteen spent nine months and heaven knows how much money to get his single, "Born to Run," to sound as if it came out of a car radio in 1958. About the same time in the 1970s pinball machine manufacturers began shifting to computers for their machines. The computers were noiseless, so the manufacturers had to install a tape recorder that played back "authentic" pinball noises. The point is technology shapes everything it touches.

The other effect of the transformation of the music into big business is a modified Steamroller, which states that the big recording companies are not so dumb as to forget that many of the biggest hits have come from the smallest places. As we have seen, the blues and early rock had an almost organic nature—they grew and were nurtured regionally before they moved into the national limelight. But in the last decade, in order for the record business to rise at a rate greater than inflation and the boredom threshold of a bunch of teenagers, new stars—*superstars*—had to be unearthed almost daily. Andy Warhol's dictum of "everyone a star for five minutes" had become the marching order for the day.

Consequently, record companies began monitoring the countryside for the first sprout of *marketable* talent. Whenever they found something that might conceivably make a trend, they plucked it and merchandized it unmercifully. The business also showed amazing adaptability, akin to the Chinese culture's ability to absorb its conquerers century after century. Many of the most successful trends of the 1970s, including Philadelphia soul, disco, punk/New Wave rock, and West Coast "soft" rock, began as reactions to the musical mainstream, originally aimed at a splinter group. The business seized each of these minority trends—after they had shown some commercial potential—and rammed them into the mainstream, pushing them for all they were worth. Unfortunately, the result has been a weakening of the music itself, just as Elvis Presley's move from regional Sun Records to national RCA portended the end of rock's violent awakening. When the stakes are raised, the game gets more conservative.

For the white boy who sang the blues, the decade began on a high note and rose to a crescendo in 1975. Within a few short years, though, that white boy had become a joke, a caricature of himself in a stained white John Travolta disco suit, marching to a passé drummer with a washed-up beat. This is what happened.

Predictably, the decade opened in Detroit and Memphis, but only for a wake. In fact, wakes were everywhere. The Beatles were wrapping things up with "Let It Be," Simon and Garfunkel were closing a long career with "Bridge over Troubled Water," and Creedance Clearwater Revival—the group that appropriated the Sun Sound and made it work on 1960s AM radio—was clearly on the ropes. In Memphis soul music had run its course; ditto for Motown in Detroit. While the Jackson Five were still going strong (as were Diana Ross and Stevie Wonder), the Motown formula had begun to fray around the edges. Times had changed, and the old formulas no longer guaranteed success.

However, two important things were beginning to happen. In Memphis Isaac Hayes, long a fixture of that city's music scene, was writing the theme for a movie about a black private detective named John Shaft, and in Philadelphia two Motown refugees, Kenny Gamble and Leon Huff, were forging a new formula, Motown for the 1970s.

The real beginning of the music scene in Philadelphia can be dated rather specifically to August 5, 1957. On that day *American Bandstand,* soon to be hosted by the ever-smiling Dick Clark and beamed to the waiting world from the depths of Philadelphia, was first broadcast. What Dick Clark brought to pop music was a squeaky-clean image; he was nothing like those sleazoid singers from Down South and Out West. *American Bandstand* became an arbiter of taste and, predictably, record companies sprang up in Philadelphia to feed on the glow from Dick Clark's teeth.

Eventually, Philadelphia built up a body of musicians who serviced these record companies, grinding out hits behind Chubby Checker, Bobby Rydell, Frankie Avalon,

Fabian, the Orlons, the Dovells, and numerous other lesser-known Philly groups. In the mid-1960s, following the glowing example of Berry Gordy at Motown, two veterans of the Philadelpia music scene, Kenny Gamble and Leon Huff, launched their own production company.

The duo scored some initial success with an old rhythm and blues vocal harmony group, the Intruders, their first signing. In 1967 they got their first national hit with the Soul Survivors' "Expressway to Your Heart," which sounded odd but upbeat on a chart dominated by soul and psychedelia. It wasn't until the late 1960s, though, that Gamble and Huff began to get a feel for what they really wanted to do. They continued to lean heavily on the local musicians, who had cut their professional teeth on in-between rock although they preferred more sophisticated jazz, but borrowed a page from Motown to write their own formula. The tricky part was avoiding too black a sound *and* too Motown or too Stax a sound at the same time. The black-music-for-white-folks market had been hit pretty heavily in the late 1960s, but Gamble and Huff correctly perceived that the largely white audience was *tired,* filled to the brim with mock gospel exhortations. So they forged a series of rhythm-and-blues–styled ballads, leaning heavily on lush orchestrations to counterpoint a punchy, almost Stax-styled rhythm section. The hits began with the Intruders' "Cowboys to Girls" in 1968, and by 1970 the Philadelphia Sound was a living, breathing thing.

The man who defined the Philadelphia Sound was Jerry Butler, originally the lead singer for the Impressions (along with Curtis Mayfield) in the late 1950s. Butler had had more downs than ups, surfacing for a hit now and again and then quickly fading. In 1969 he released "Only the Strong Survive," written by himself, Gamble, and Huff, and it became an immediate hit. This was the prototypical Philly record—a smooth, almost hypnotic vocal track over a tough rhythm section, sweetened by lush orchestration. Each subsequent single showed Gamble and Huff increasingly in control of their creation, and they had such diverse hits as Archie Bell's "I Can't Stop Dancing" and Dusty Springfield's "Brand New Me." In 1971 the newly formed Philadelphia International, distributed by canny CBS Records, which saw the new wave coming, took off like a truckload of rockets. Within the next few years Philly International, riding such artists as the O'Jays ("Back Stabbers," "Love Train," "For the Love of Money," "Put Your Hands Together"), Billy Paul ("Me and Mrs. Jones"), Harold Melvin and the Blue Notes ("If You Don't Know Me by Now," "Satisfaction Guaranteed," "Wake Up Everybody"), and the Three Degrees ("When Will I See You Again"), began to dominate the charts, and by 1975 the Philly Sound reigned supreme—just as Motown had in the 1960s.

Gamble and Huff weren't the only ones producing the music—in fact, their most successful stylist became their most successful competitor. Thom Bell took the Gamble and Huff formula to rarified heights with the Stylistics ("You Are Everything," "Betcha by Golly Wow," "Break Up to Make Up"), the Delfonics ("La La Means I Love You," "Didn't I," "Hey Love"), and the Spinners, Motown veterans who produced some of the finest Philly music, including "I'll Be Around," "Could It Be I'm Falling in Love," and "One of a Kind (Love Affair)." It almost seemed that any artist could come to Philly, turn himself over to either of the masters, and record a quick hit. The Philly formula was the perfect foil for the harder rock music of the times (which had diversified wildly, from Alice Cooper to Roxy Music), and once again Philadelphia seemed to have its finger on the pulse of America.

What caused that pulse to skip a beat, and made the Philadelphia masters rich while diluting their music, had to do with what Isaac Hayes was doing in Memphis while Gamble and Huff were making Motown for the 1970s. Hayes, together with a funky rhythm and blues studio in Miami, was creating disco music.

Basically, Philadelphia music was, as one critic caustically wrote, rhythm and blues without the rhythm and without the blues. All that was left was the passion. It was a strange passion, without sweat, one step removed from even Motown, which was already one step removed from gospel fervor. Philly soul was to soul what doo-wop was to rhythm and blues—*acceptable* black music, without the sweaty taint of the soul man or the indescribable gospel highs of Motown. To mainstream white America, Philly soul was another in a series of proofs that, really, they're just like us. They make up to break up and have a lot of trouble saying "I love you." Philly soul expressed black America's longing for acceptance. More bluntly, it spelled surrender. The smashing success of Philly soul in the mid-1970s proved that the beat went on, but it had left a lot behind.

In 1971 the runaway hit of the year came, once again, from Memphis, but it was unlike anything else that city had produced in its long musical history. The song was

"Shaft," written by Isaac Hayes, a veteran Stax composer, arranger, producer, and artist. Hayes and David Porter had written some of Stax's most memorable material, including Sam and Dave's "Soul Man," "Hold On, I'm Coming," "I Thank You," and many, many others. Hayes had shown a penchant for more sophisticated material with his long, soul-dripping version of Dionne Warwick's "Walk On By" in 1969 and his similar restyling of Glen Campbell's "By the Time I Get to Phoenix" the next year. With "Shaft," though, he intended something different, his own updated version of rhythm and blues for the urban landscape. Released in August of 1971, the song was a phenomenal success, the fastest-selling record in the history of Stax Records. It went gold in three weeks, platinum by the end of October. The record was absolutely hypnotic, an infectious, danceable rhythm track overlaid with perfect orchestration and Hayes' mellow soul-man voice. An R & B dance record overlaid with orchestration, "Shaft" proved to be the wave of the future.

If "Shaft" was the first example of disco music (and still one of the finest), there were other equally powerful portents that year. Betty Wright, a former gospel singer and local star in the Miami area, hit the national charts with "Clean Up Woman," another get-up-and-boogie rhythm and blues performance. Less sophisticated (some would say less overblown) than the Hayes masterpiece, "Clean Up Woman" was still a clear sign that something was cooking, and not only in Philadelphia.

Actually, things were brewing all over the place, especially in Miami and New York City. The reaction to the oh-so-political 1960s had finally set in: the white nigger had given way to the cool spade; Eldridge Cleaver was out, Superfly was in. People no longer wanted to smash the state, they wanted to have a good time—they wanted to dance. In New York City, especially in the gay ghettoes, the smooth sounds of Philadelphia had been integrated onto the dance floors. With a song like "Shaft" a person could really *move* the body, and not in the stoned shaking and quaking that passed for dancing in the 1960s, but in a stylized dance with real, complicated steps. A dance that looked suspiciously like black dances, if the truth be told. Black dance never did break down altogether in the epileptic 1960s; Gladys Knight and the Pips always did a killer stage routine, even when it drew sniggers from the audience. In the gay ghettoes, where emphasis on the body was paramount, those slicked-up routines looked good on a dance floor—no sniggers there.

The problem, at least initially, was finding material to dance to. Philly International's songs were snapped up quickly, and Gamble and Huff and Thom Bell were quick to capitalize on the new dance craze. They began expanding their material to accommodate the dance disc jockeys, but still the music lacked a really punchy rhythm that would *make* the people get up and dance. That rhythm was finally supplied by the home of Clean Up Woman Betty Wright—Miami.

Wright's hit was on tiny Alston Records, one of a series of small labels tied into TK recording studios on the outskirts of Miami. Miami had impeccable soul credentials. The distinctive beats of the nearby Caribbean Islands blended well with the music of numerous expatriate soul men, many of them imported by Atlantic Records godfather Jerry Wexler to work at Criteria Studio in Miami. In the early 1970s that studio sported one of the most famous and accomplished house bands in the country, the Dixie Flyers, featuring Jim Dickinson and the legendary Charlie Freemen, two mainstays of the Memphis white boys scene. In addition, Miami had the rarest of all the ingredients necessary to make the formula work—clubs, nightclubs, honky-tonks, places where musicians could make a living while hammering out a style.

In 1974 disco bubbled out of the gay ghettoes to sweep the country in a storm that rivaled the introduction of the Twist in the early 1960s. This instantaneous success was possible because a record could become a hit in the discos without any airplay on radio. This phenomenon opened up a whole new market for the record companies, which they were quick to exploit to the hilt. The first big disco hit to cross over to radio (in the summer of 1974) was "Rock the Boat" by a Las Vegas lounge group called the Hues Corporation. It was followed the next month by George McCrae's "Rock Your Baby," straight from Miami.

The genius behind "Rock Your Baby" was the songwriting team of Harry Casey and Rick Finch, who would quickly become K.C. and the Sunshine Band. In the summer of 1975 K.C. and the Sunshine Band dominated the charts, beginning with "Get Down Tonight" and going through a series of hard-ass, dance-to-it hits like "That's the Way (I Like It)," "Queen of Clubs," and "Shake, Shake, Shake, Your Booty." The Miami music galvanized the disco scene and the inescapable rhythms of K.C. drove disco into every corner of the country.

Here is the irony: Just as Philadelphia soul was rhythm and blues without the rhythm or the blues, music from T.K. Studios, especially K.C. and the Sunshine Band, was soul music without the soul man.

Does it come as any surprise that Harry Casey and

Rick Finch, the leaders of the most successful rhythm and blues band in the 1970s, are white? Again, we find the same dichotomy as in the Motown-Stax push-pull of the 1960s and the rock and roll–rhythm and blues fights of the 1950s. In black-controlled Philly music, as in black-controlled Motown, the trend is always toward respectability, away from the blues. Of course, exceptions can be cited, but the predominant trend in black music since the turn of the century has been toward the mainstream, away from those cottonfield darkies. Conversely, the trend in popular (read: white) music has been toward the minority. Minority trends are quickly processed into the majority, and just as quickly discarded. Down through the years, time and time again, the most viable, most dynamic, most powerful, most *earthshaking* crossbreed has been the white man singing the blues, the black/white cross.

The high-water mark for disco came in 1977 with the release of *Saturday Night Fever,* a film based loosely on a *New York* magazine article on the "new" young people. The movie, starring teen idol John Travolta, was sort of about growing up, disco style, the relationship between a young man, a young woman, and a vitally important way of life–the dance floor. Like the best rock and roll or the best popular art of any kind, the movie both defined and explained its times.

It also marked the zenith of the white boy singing the blues. Here was John Travolta, painfully Italian, in his white disco suit (courtesy of *Superfly*) with his cool spade moves and his ghetto argot, dancing black-styled dances (the Cootie Crawl would have been right at home on the dance floor) to the Bee Gees' rendition of disco music. The Bee Gees, no less–an Australian group that had first found favor during the British Invasion of the early 1960s and now returned for a mini-invasion of their own. The Bee Gees took the T.K. style (which they had picked up in Miami, to their credit), filed off the rough edges, and produced the biggest-selling album in the history of popular music. *Saturday Night Fever* said it all, without pretense and without guile: the white boy singing the blues had finally displaced blacks altogether. Even as the movie reveled in its borrowed "blackness" and its white/black/white music, the record companies took the predictable next step. They softened-up the music some more and *shoved* hard. They recycled old groups and old hits. Motown benefited especially, since the Motown style was easily adapted to the Philly slick disco formula. But all the while John Travolta danced, a backlash was building, and the triumph of Motown over Stax was to be surprisingly short-lived.

THE REACTION

For the first time, American pop music doesn't seem to make a bow to black music.

—Linda Ronstadt, *Playboy*

Disco Sucks!
—Popular slogan, circa 1979

It happened so fast the whole thing could have been missed with a single inopportune blink. One minute the whole world loves a white suit, the next disco is passé, yesterday's trend. Disc jockeys make their reputations with "Disco Sucks!" parties; bumper stickers and T-shirts echo the sentiment. Discos either close down or shift to more rock and roll or old rock and roll or even country music—*anything* but disco. Record company executives who piously proclaimed disco as the wave of the 1980s now piously claim to have been the first to spot its demise. Disco artists find themselves both unemployed and unemployable. Disco movies are released, only to sink without a trace.

The Reaction is in. The Reaction is the cultural equivalent of the much vaunted "white backlash" of the early 1970s. The music that replaces disco on the dance floor and on the radio is not necessarily more dynamic or more pure (whatever that means) or more original than disco. If there is any common denominator, it is that the music is more, well, *white*. The reaction is not so much to disco (or to the bloated bodies of the record companies or even to the superstar groups that can dominate the charts if they choose), but to the supremacy of the white boy singing the blues. Having now totally assimilated his version of black culture over a period of three decades, the white boy is faced with an interesting question: Who *do* you think you are?

Puzzled, the white boy has no answer. He has forgotten from where he swiped the clothes and the moves and the talk. He has been told, and now believes, that the music came either from him, which is not true, or from "the blacks," which is also not true. It has slipped his mind that the gallant talk of the disco—"My Lady" this, "My Lady" that—is the argot of black pimps, grease to ease the transition into The Life. The only roots he remembers are Alex Haley's. Who indeed does he think he is?

While John Travolta was dancing, the most overt part of the Reaction was also dancing, but to a music called New Wave. New Wave music first surfaced in New York City around 1976, the outgrowth of that city's booming and sometimes bizarre musical scene. Its antecedents were such groups as the New York Dolls and the Velvet

Underground. In England, where a similar movement developed independently, the roots were in that country's pub bands, analogous perhaps to the bar bands that preceded the birth of rock in America in the 1950s. What New Wave music was (or is, depending on how wide one is willing to spread the definition) was primitive rock, basic three-chord rock and roll or rockabilly, new-sounding, raunchy, and incredibly vital compared to the run-of-the-mill music on the radio. One could dance any kind of dance one wanted to it, or just stand there and be bowled over by the noise. Two words came to symbolize the new music. The first was "fun," usually applied to the three-minute ultraloud ditties by groups like the Ramones, from the American branch of the family, which tended to concentrate on girls, sex, cars, sex, beaches, sex, and teenage angst. The second was "dangerous," applied only to the English cousins such as the notorious Sex Pistols or, more recently, the Clash. As an aside, British punk/New Wave did indeed rise out of the working-class pubs and was firmly rooted in a working-class antiauthoritarian or overtly antigovernment posture, as exemplified in the Sex Pistols' "God Save the Queen." Despite much whining by critics, however, the political ramifications of New Wave never meant much in America, where, in fact, those very ramifications hindered the acceptance of the new music. And the political posturing of the English groups was tempered by their success in the marketplace. It's hard to make a million bucks and continue to worry about the plight of the working man.

The cliché is that New Wave rose out of disgust with the domination of the airways by a few large groups, such as the Who and the Rolling Stones and the Eagles.

While there is clearly an element of truth in that explanation, it overlooks the fact that those groups were at the top because they were exactly what the public wanted. Sure, there was and is a lot of stale music, but as science fiction writer Norman Spinrad said, "Eighty percent of all science fiction is shit. For that matter, though, 80 percent of *everything* is shit!" The Who were doing some of their most vital work in those years; the Rolling Stones had just staged a major comeback; and *Saturday Night Fever* had changed the entire dynamics of the record business. Yes, the groups made truckloads of money, didn't tour often, and played to the biggest crowds they could get. But so did the Beatles and so did Elvis Presley.

I think the real answer to the rise of New Wave music lies in the Reaction itself. New Wave music is self-consciously *white*. The beat moved on, and New Wave is an attempt to redefine music without it. "For the first time, American pop music doesn't seem to make a bow to black music—except reggae, which is Third World music," said Linda Ronstadt, the reigning Queen of West Coast (soft) Rock, in *Playboy* magazine. "For a while it was very much an in thing for white musicians to be able to play with heavy black affectations; for instance, putting the rhythm emphasis way back behind the beat. If you could do that and keep the groove, that was a real hip thing to do, and now it's the opposite. The grooves are very rushed and very fast and the emphasis seems to be very much on top of the beat. The moves I see are very white. I saw the B-52s and their moves, well, they look like something in a Holiday Inn disco, sort of Ohio housewife dancing—very white."

A word on reggae is in order. Reggae is Jamaican soul music, which grew out of Jamaican pop music called ska.

Ska (the word itself is a vocal approximation of the sound their guitars made) grew up in the early 1960s when island musicians grafted their own distinctive rhythms, called *mento*, onto New Orleans rhythm and blues. The graft came about because New Orleans' radio stations boomed into Jamaica at night, and the musicians liked what they heard. The resulting music was light and fast, dominated by saxophones and trombones. Television and movie themes were recut in ska versions, and one ska tune, "My Boy Lollipop," by Millie Small, even made the American charts in 1964 (most thought it was yet another weirdness from England).

Ska eventually gave way to rock steady, a slower musical form that better lent itself to dancing than the frenetic ska. Rock steady, in turn, sped up and picked up a stronger rhythm track to become reggae. Since the early 1970s reggae has been continually billed as the Next Big Thing, and a couple of reggae songs have even made the charts, albeit in diluted forms (most notably Paul Simon's "Mother and Child Reunion," Eric Clapton's "I Shot the Sheriff," Johnny Nash's "I Can See Clearly Now," and Jimmy Cliff's "Wonderful World, Beautiful People)." The biggest superstars of reggae, Bob Marley and the Wailers and Toots and the Maytals, have consistently failed to penetrate the American market despite widespread publicity, tours, and pushes from bigger acts.

The reasons are fairly obvious. Critics latched on to reggae because it was "authentic" black music, untouched by *the* white taint. It was also exotic, which has, in the past, always helped to make black music more palatable. But the critics' viewpoint was erroneously based on the assumption that American popular music was shaped by blacks rather than by the clash of black and white. Ska is having its greatest effect (which isn't much) on the American market through a New Wave revival by such groups as the Specials, the Madness, and the English Beat. Perhaps the revival of ska means the beginning of a whole new cycle of white boys singing the blues.

The biggest winner in the Reaction has been country music. So far the greatest trend of the budding 1980s has not been New Wave, reggae, neo-disco, or what-have-you, but the stunning rise of country music. Willie Nelson, the venerable Texas institution, emerged as one of the biggest superstars of the late 1970s, nudging aside all who stood in his way. The record charts, which had begun to open up to New Wave–styled acts, are now dominated by "new" country music à la Charlie Daniels and Kenny Rogers. Country nightclubs are opening faster than discos (sometimes as country discos) with amazing success. And John Travolta has been reincarnated as the Urban Cowboy.

That the movie *Urban Cowboy* stiffed at the box office hardly diminishes its importance. It filled the void left by the collapse of the white boy singing the blues; it offered white kids a way to be hip without being black. Instead of being a *white* boy, one could become a *cow*boy. So jeans and western shirts have replaced white suits, Texas drawl the ghetto argot, and, for a while at least, America seems content to wallow in its *other* favorite myth, that of the cowboy.

Of course, country music itself has never been that far from black music, and many recent country hits ("Stand by Me," by Mickey Gilley, for example, from the film *Urban Cowboy*) are reworkings of old soul numbers. It seems that black and white are too entwined to ever sort out completely.

Originally, new music came about because of the relationships and interactions between musicians and between the musicians and their surrounding societies. From the days of the spirituals through early country music to rhythm and blues, we found the music subtly shifting along the currents of black and white, with the musicians all borrowing from one another and then changing what they took to fit the times and the places. In rock and roll we see the cataclysmic fusing of black and white, not through design, but through the social forces at work in places like Memphis and Macon and throughout the South. In Memphis we see a musical continuum that stretches from the earliest days of the city to the present.

What sets the new rock apart from the old is its hopeless pretension, which seems to gnaw at everything that is being accomplished musically. This pretension says, "Look at me. I can do this better than the originals, because the originals are nothing but a bunch of old niggers/old rednecks, and what do they know?"

I'm reminded of Michael Bloomfield's comment when Brian Jones of the Rolling Stones told him that "the Rolling Stones are really a blues group." Bloomfield's reply was something along the lines of "If you say so, whatever." In the new world of rock and roll you are what you say you are. The cover of the new Clash album carries a sticker that reads, "18 songs from the only band that matters," and a review of the album modestly proclaims that "Clash music embraces all that's vital in rock and roll and black music of the last 20 years."

"If you say so" are the new bywords. The white man no longer needs to sing the blues, he simply *says* he sings them, and, *ergo,* it's true. This is the ultimate extension of the great British terminology raid of the early 1960s. That's why a New Wave group like the Cramps can go to Memphis to record an album (because of the ambiance of the city) and then announce at a news conference, "Elvis Presley was the king of rock and roll, and now he's dead, and I believe that the Cramps are the new kings— and queen—of rock and roll." No doubt there are kids out there who think that that press conference is only slightly less authentic than the Ten Commandments.

This is the mentality that turns the Blues Brothers into monster hits—imitation is not only a safe refuge, it allows you to vent emotions that are usually held in check. It's a good joke, them funny-looking guys imitating niggers and all. But they're white—get it?

I happened to see John Belushi (the bluesy half) at the New York City comeback concert of the Allman Brothers Band. He came onstage to join the Allmans during one of their many encores, and I thought back to the Atlanta Pop Festival, almost a decade before, when a lot of other people had joined the Brothers onstage. But with Belushi it was different, almost a question of generation gap—or the new, improved product meeting the old original item. It was awkward and embarrassing, and the crowd loved every minute of it.

That the old rock—the black/white fusion—retains its power after all these years is evidenced by its imitators. The music of Memphis—the blues, rockabilly, and soul— plays a huge part in New Wave music. More than that, the old rock still has a way of sneaking up on people and clouting them over the head. John Prine is best known as a somewhat sensitive Vietnam War era folkie, author of such songs as "Hello in There" and "Sam Stone." After a brief affair with Nashville, Prine was directed to Memphis to cut his new album by none other than "Cowboy" Jack Clement, a Nashville fixture who once produced Jerry Lee Lewis at Sun Records. Go to Memphis, "Cowboy" told Prine, and just listen to what's there. Prine did exactly that, and was floored.

"It was the most spiritual place I've ever been," Prine told me one afternoon in New York City. "It almost seems like there's a wall around the place. It was incredible."

Prine fell in with Jerry and Knox Phillips, Sam's sons, who worked at the old Phillips Recording Studio. Soon Sam himself showed up, unable to stay away.

"The first night recording, all the knobs fell off the equipment, some of it started smoking, and Knox and Jerry started talking real seriously about ghosts," Prine said. Soon the three Phillipses were running upstairs and retrieving old Sun tapes, most of which Prine had never heard. The result was an album entitled *Pink Cadillac,* and it did the same thing as the Allman Brothers' first music—it redefined the old fusions in a modern context. It was a good modern album without pretensions, without posturing, but with a definite sense of roots, black and white. Because it refused to fit into any niche, it almost goes without saying that *Pink Cadillac* was a failure on the charts.

"Listen," says John Prine, "I know that this album is totally foreign to what other people are doing. But I know I'm right. I *know* I'm *right.* People don't have to buy the record to prove that to me."

We are not who we think we are . . .

I am at a party in Manhattan, and I am trapped in a

corner. The predator is a young woman in her twenties, wearing black spandex jeans and an old man's shirt with a skinny tie. She demands to know whether I am indeed writing a book on black music and white music.

"Sort of," I say, as noncommittally as possible.

"Then you know about reggae," she says and I agree.

"Did you know that ska bands in England actually have black and white members, playing together?" she asks.

"No kidding."

"That's right, black and white," she says, her eyes glowing with evangelical fervor. "They're doing what no other music has ever *dared* to do, put black and white together."

"Just like brothers?" I ask timidly.

"Just like brothers," she affirms.

There is a moment of silence while I debate telling her about rock and roll, the white blues kids, rockabilly, the Allman Brothers, the spirituals, whatever. I finally decide to keep my mouth shut.

"That's what's wrong with the *old* music," she says, warming to the subject. "They didn't know *shit* about soul, real *soul.* But pretty soon blacks and whites are going to be together because of the music, because they play in bands together and stuff."

"No kidding," I say again, incredulous. "Well, I'll be damned."

"You put that in your book," she concludes, and I do.

EPILOGUE: A WHITE BOY SINGING THE BLUES

The heat shimmers off the cracked pavement of Beale Street like a ghostly curtain, and through the gauze curtain come flashes of crowds, the shouts of pawnshop hawkers, snatches of the blues. The reality is entirely different. A green sign, placed by the city of Memphis, reads, "You Are Now Crossing World Famous Beale Street," and the view is something like that in Dresden, Germany, after the bombings of World War II. The area for miles around has been bulldozed flat and is covered with a layer of dying grass, which gives the remaining four blocks of Beale Street an eerie air, like something out of a science fiction novel. Or, more accurately, like something from a trashed-out Disney Film—four blocks of crumbling buildings, the windows covered with brightly painted plywood while the turn-of-the-century façades rot and crumble, all surrounded by acres and acres of what appears to be parkland. Closest to the river, where the magnificent sidewheel riverboats used to dock to unload their bales of cotton and thousands of visitors to the bright lights of the city, a thick layer of asphalt covers the cobblestones laid by slave labor just before the Civil War. A trendy restaurant housed in a converted cotton ware-house looks out over the river, guarding the dead en-trance to Beale. The fish market at Beale and Front Street, once the best in the South, has given way to a parking lot, and Main Street, in the next block, has been repaved and turned into a walking arcade—although there is precious little reason to stroll there. Once there was a record store on Main, just a few storefronts off Beale Street, called the Home of the Blues, that so im-pressed the young Johnny Cash and his co-writer, Vic McAlpine, that they couldn't help but write a song about it, and the title of the song is, of course, "Home of the Blues."

Along the street that losers use there is now a huge sign, erected by the city of Memphis, and covered with dust on this blistering summer day: BEALE STREET WILL LIVE AGAIN. TOGETHER, WE ARE REBUILDING THE HOME OF THE BLUES.

Precious little else is alive on the street. Most of the old shops are closed. All the pawnshops with their three golden balls and windows full of shattered dreams have left for less fertile ground. The Pantaze Drugstore is closed, and, above it, the Club Handy sits empty and forsaken. The honky-tonks and restaurants and flop-houses are gone—most owners didn't even bother to relo-cate, just closed their doors and walked away. A few held their ground: Lansky Brothers Clothing, where Elvis got his pink suits and, before him, where all the hep cats did their shopping, is still there. My high school knock-around buddy Shelby bought his clothes at Lansky's (those that he didn't make himself). Although he was white, he was given to wearing yellow-and-black-checked suits with high-heeled patent leather boots. At first, Shelby seemed oblivious of the snickers when he strutted down Beale Street, a white peacock interrupting the dance. Like Elvis, his clothes were more important to him than the snickers—they were a key element in staying alive while totally out of his element. The breaking point came one summer afternoon near the corner of Beale and Main, when six white sailors decided that while busting up a black on Beale Street might be suicidal, busting up a weirdly dressed white kid was as safe and easy as attending a church luncheon. Shelby also wore a chrome-plated logging chain, and when the dust settled, Shelby was still standing. The next time he walked down Beale Street, there weren't any snickers, and even the black hookers had a bit of good-natured ribbing for him. For the record, Shelby was hardly your basic one-world liberal. "Actually," he said time and time again, "I'm not prejudiced against blacks. I hate everyone equally, until they give me a reason to think otherwise. And I just go ahead and do what I want to do." In those sticky summer days, before an assassin's bullet echoed along Beale Street to strike at the nearby Lorraine Motel and seal the street's fate, there was still room for a crazy white kid, just as there had been in the 1950s.

Peter Guralnick, who has managed to spend so much time in Memphis that his friends refer to him as a de facto Memphian, once did an interview with Charlie Feathers in which Charlie spoke at length and with readily apparent love for his black mentors. One of Charlie's kids interrupted the interview, and in the course of that conversation Charlie told Peter that he didn't want his kids to be bused to school with a bunch of niggers.

After much thought and more than a little soul searching, Peter's conclusion was that, ultimately, there was no contradiction in the two halves of Charlie Feathers' conversation—just like Sam Phillips, distressed at the plight of the black in the South, starting his own recording studio to record black music rather than join a crusade or social movement, only to move on to recording white acts when he perceived that black musicians had other reliable outlets.

Look at my friend Shelby, walking down Beale Street in his yellow plaid suit. *I'm not prejudiced,* he says, *I hate everybody. The only thing that matters is the individual.*

That is the central theme in Memphis: *only the individual matters.* That allows a white man to support segregation, to support racism, while having a profound admiration, even a love, for individual blacks. It allows dealings to take place on a level *other* than race. There *was* a level of interaction between blacks and whites in Memphis that overrode racial barriers. It was a spontaneous and totally genuine interchange, and while it didn't necessarily lead to a greater understanding between the races, it led to rock and roll and to soul music. White men singing the blues, or at least pumping away in the rhythm section.

That's what makes it so damn hard to understand, hard even for me to write about. *You're a closet racist,* a voice in the back of my head keeps nagging. *You have not purged your soul of racial hatred.* Of course, there are no real answers.

We stare back at Memphis through twenty-five years

of racial upheaval, and we can't help seeing snarling police dogs and truncheons or a small group of men standing on the balcony of the Lorraine Motel, pointing to an invisible assassin. At night, after the assassination, you could hear gunfire from across town, and the next morning I sneaked past the National Guard checkpoints to go downtown and see for myself the burned buildings and shattered glass along Beale Street. Up and down the street were the littered posters from the march the day before. "I Am A Man," the posters read.

It has been the better part of a decade since Archie Bunker first muttered the forbidden word "nigger" on our television sets and in our living rooms, and since then we have embraced soft-core racism and at the same time walked over the minefield of racism on our tippy toes, desperately afraid of giving the appearance of being an "Archie Bunker." We now see racism under every bed, the way our fathers in the McCarthy Era saw communists. Robert Christgau, the music editor of *The Village Voice*, recently wondered in print whether a dislike of disco music wasn't perhaps racially motivated, whether the overwhelming rejection of disco by music critics might be based on color rather than quality.

And so we look on Memphis with distaste, because we live in an age of post-liberalism. The great social movements of the 1960s, when we wholeheartedly adopted black music, black argot, and what we thought was black thinking, are dead and gone to dust. Being poor got boring. Calling everyone brother and sister just didn't make it in the Me Decade. We began to worry about whether our school districts were "good," meaning free of poor Negroes, or "bad," meaning that half the third-grade class carried knives. In short, we have gone through a

complete reversal, adopting exactly the opposite attitudes of Sam Phillips and the people in Memphis. We
have become semantic egalitarians, and we find the appearance of racism distasteful. Like the hapless rock critic
who struggles to like a music because it is black rather
than because it is good, we *want* to grasp what happened
in Memphis, but it refuses to conform to our precon-
ceived notions. What we would like to believe is that,
somehow, the vicious racial pressures of the ·South had
been lifted in Memphis, and that, hand in hand, black
and white had gone on to create some of the most important music ever produced in America. We want to think
that everybody loved everybody else, that Elvis was a
member of the SCLC and Sam Phillips started his own
Anti-Defamation League. We demand to know why
blues singers didn't resemble Bob Dylan in blackface,
singing searing protest music that drove the plantation
owners back in panic, their hands over their ears.

We look back on what happened in Memphis from our
unbearably smug perspective, like the Swedish journalist
who came to the city to write the definitive history of the
Memphis blues and asked everybody he talked to for
photographs. Then he kept the photographs, since those
"poor old colored people" didn't realize the importance
of what they had. Like the first Memphis Blues Festival
in 1969, when earnest young white kids were encouraged
to perform, showing how they'd learned and, indeed, ex-
panded upon the blues, while great pains were made to
keep Stax "soul" artists from being involved. After all,
they weren't "pure" black music, the white kids reasoned. Like Janis Joplin coming to Memphis for her cor-
onation, then leaving the stage in a fury when it didn't
happen.

We look back on Memphis smug in our knowledge
that we now love blacks as a race, but hate individual
Negroes, and we are chagrined that such cultural earth-
quakes have come from such a backward redneck racist
backwater.

The pattern should be obvious by now—the great
waves in popular music have come from the often bitter,
always cataclysmic smashing of black against white. To
insist, as does LeRoi Jones and his many supporters, that
the white man stole from the black man is to purposely
screen out what really happened and do a disservice to
both black and white.

Whites *did* steal something from blacks. They swiped
an imaginary culture, based on snatches of rhythm and
blues songs and cool black cats in cheap black movies.
White kids based their "culture" on the fact that they
were niggers, niggers who wanted to live in a tribe and
relate on some basis other than language. They called
each other "brother" and "sister" and "blood," practiced
the handshakes of the ghetto, and tried real hard to get
close to "authentic" niggers.

They did this because—this is my guess, and I'm afraid
a guess is all that it is—white kids simply could not find
any other way to relate to black kids. The old relationship had been shattered, and, unfortunately, that included the good in it as well as the millions of bad things.
Phil Walden pointed to the collapse of the personal relationship between southern blacks and whites as one of
the symptoms. The rise of black consciousness ended the
one-on-one relationships that had punctuated southern
life for years. And from the collapse of the old relationships came a whole new spiral of racism—"If he don't

want nothing to do with me, I don't want nothing to do with him."

I should pause here to acknowledge that much about the old black-white relationship was nightmarish. But there *were* personal relationships that transcended racism—I had some, and I'm a lesser person now because they're gone. I don't think those relationships had anything to do with racism or bulldozing the blacks. They gave both of us the chance to peer into a different world, to see the events of the day through different eyes, to understand that there *was* another side. Once those relationships ended, imitation seemed the only alternative.

Early last year I got a phone call from a friend in San Francisco who said he had a magazine assignment to go to Memphis and find the blues, or what was left of them. He was calling to see if I had any names he could call when he got to town. "Forget it," I said. "Nobody in town talks to outsiders." But he persisted, and I gave him some names and wished him luck. When the article appeared in *Mother Jones* magazine, my friend managed to touch the heart of the matter, although nobody talked to him in Memphis: "I was white, but black people had given America almost everything in it that I loved— blues, jazz, gospel, jitterbug dancing, red beans and rice, hot barbecue, blaxploitation movies, most of the good slang, street funerals, gumbo, Motown, and sweet potato pie. Most of my heroes were black, from Marie Laveau to Lester Young, Martin Luther King to Angela Davis."

In an encounter with a black hitchhiker, though, his search for the blues was temporarily derailed. The hitchhiker went to the disco and smoked dope. "This wasn't working out right. . . . He was supposed to hit me with a hip handshake and say, 'Hey, man, les you and me make

it over to de juke joint down by de river, where they be
playin' them good old-time blues. Doin' usually let no
white mens in, but *you* pretty hip.' But he didn't care if I
was hip, just that I was white."

"You can't imitate black people," says Jim Dickinson.
"Although I've seen a lot of people try. We had people
move down here, playing music and trying to live like a
nigger, thinking that was what it was all about. Well,
that's not ever what it was all about. I'll tell you, about
the biggest compliment I ever got in my life was at one of
the blues festivals, and I'd been playing like a demon. As
I was walking offstage, I saw Bukka White—one of the
really great bluesmen—and he was laughing. 'Shit,' he
said, 'it's been a long time since I heard anybody play
like that, black or white. Boy, I bet you got a bit of the
twist in you.' Maybe I was a little black, he was saying,
and I thought, goddam, maybe I am."

We sit on his couch pawing through pictures of what
he laughingly calls the "old days," the wild and woolly
days of the early 1970s. Trips on the road with the Rolling Stones, movie deals, big-time recording contracts in
Los Angeles, wild times with the Dixie Flyers—sort of a
shoebox full of the music of the 1970s. What he is trying
to explain to me, with the help of pictures, is why he
decided to return to Memphis, despite the promise of
even bigger successes elsewhere.

Sure, he knows a musician could *starve* to death in
Memphis. Always been that way, probably always will
be that way. He knows all the standard jokes, too: That
about three-quarters of Nashville's much-vaunted country music industry consists of expatriate Memphians.
Chips Moman from Stax turned Waylon Jennings' career
around. Jack Clement, the *other* producer at Sun Rec-

ords, scored ten gold records with Charlie Pride and engineered Johnny Cash's spectacular comeback in recent years. Sun veteran Allen Reynolds masterminded the rise of Crystal Gayle. The list goes on and on. The strength of the famed Muscle Shoals rhythm section lies on the shoulders of Memphians who couldn't find work in their home city.

But James Luther Dickinson came back to live in a farmhouse about thirty miles from Beale Street, to raise his two kids within spitting distance of the blues. The house is comfortable, the kind of place city people imagine when they talk about "moving to the country" and "getting back to the roots." It is about as off the beaten path as you can get without living on an island. "Naw, it's no problem to find," he said earlier, over the telephone. "Just take a left turn and go until you get to the first house that looks like a white person lives in it. That's me."

"Didja have any trouble finding the place?" he asks when I arrive. Nope. He laughs. "Yeah, those directions always seem to work."

No one in Memphis is quite sure what to do with James Luther, also known as (in his lighter moments) Captain Memphis. His talent is inescapable—just before leaving the supersessions' group the Dixie Flyers, he cut his own album *James Luther Dickinson*, which didn't sell. It was, however, hailed as a masterpiece, a pulling together of the seemingly divergent Memphis traditions (which he knew had never really diverged in the first place) into an outstanding and powerful record. Critic Nick Tosches called the record "one of the most bizarrely powerful musics of the century; a loud, moralless baptism of rhythm." Dickinson went on to produce the *Beale Street Saturday*

Night album, which evidenced a depth of understanding for Memphis music that is especially rare in Memphis. "It was an excuse to give money to a bunch of old black people, and I really liked doing that."

Enlightening, but it still doesn't explain what he is doing back in Memphis, on the other side of the world from rock and roll success. He gets up from the couch and paces, in his pajamas, around the living room. Two or three times he starts to speak, then shifts gears and continues pacing. Finally he walks through the dining room to a window and jerks back the shade.

"Come here," he says, and I get up and follow him to the window.

"Look out there and tell me what you see," says James Luther Dickinson.

I say, "Tenement shacks."

"Like hell," he says. "What you see is *nigger* houses, sharecroppers shacks. And, damn it, I want to be able to see those shacks. I want to be able to see those honky-tonks. There is just something in me that loves it. Now maybe that makes me a racist, I don't know. But this is like Paris at the turn of the century—we saw a change in Memphis that affected the whole world. . . . A bunch of crazy rednecks playing nigger music."

He waves his arms like a schoolteacher gone berserk, and the curtain drops back over the window.

"People don't understand the life of Elvis Presley, and people *won't* understand the life of Elvis Presley. Elvis did just what he wanted to do. He never did anything but rock and roll. He played the Ubangi Stomp till he rolled over dead. This is where I want to be."

Index

Other DACAPO titles of interest